ZONING
ITS COSTS AND RELEVANCE
FOR THE 1980s

ZONING
ITS COSTS AND RELEVANCE FOR THE 1980s

Michael Goldberg and Peter Horwood

with
Roscoe Jones and David Baxter
Walter Block (Editor)

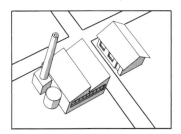

THE FRASER INSTITUTE

1980

Canadian Cataloguing in Publication Data
Goldberg, Michael A., 1941-
  Zoning, its costs and relevance for the 1980s

  (Fraser Institute housing and land economics
series ; no. 6)
  Bibliography: p.
  ISBN 0-88975-032-7

  1. Zoning. I. Horwood, Peter, 1949-
II. Block, Walter, 1941-   III. Title.
IV. Series: Fraser Institute, Vancouver, B.C.
Fraser Institute housing and land economics
series ; no. 6.
HT169.6.G64   352.9'61   C79-091240-6

Contents

FIGURES

PHOTOGRAPHS

Preface

In the view of most concerned professionals, zoning legislation is a necessary bulwark against chaos in urban land use.
Without zoning, it is contended, external diseconomies will
abound: pickle works will come to rest cheek-by-jowl with
single family homes; glue factories beside country clubs; and
oil refineries in proximity to restaurants. Moreover, it is
feared that rapacious land developers will erect, profit from,
and then abandon buildings placing undue strain on the
capacities of municipal services. Further, the unzoned city
will be one of haphazard construction, falling property
values, instability, disregard for neighborhood "character,"
irrational allocation of property - and a haven for unscrupu-
lous speculators.
    Zoning is the attempt to suppress these supposed
market defects by legislatively prohibiting incompatible uses
of land. Under this ordinance, the pickle factory would be
prohibited from residential neighborhoods and required to
locate itself in a special industrial area, reserved for that
kind of operation. There, surrounded by similar uses, it would
presumably do little harm.

The zoning idea has a certain appeal. What, after all, could be more simple and obvious? If land usage seems imperfect, all that is needed is the enactment of a set of laws compelling proper behaviour. Arguments for zoning are so widely made and frequently accepted that even those who otherwise appreciate the merits of the competitive market system have felt constrained to make an exception in this instance. In view of this state of affairs, and given the serious drawbacks in zoning which are continually making themselves felt, the Fraser Institute has undertaken this monograph, the sixth in its Housing Studies series. In it, Professor Michael A. Goldberg and Mr. Peter J. Horwood present an insightful, dispassionate analysis which questions the case for zoning legislation.

Non-zoning in Houston

Confronting the charge that zoning is all that stands between a viable urban environment and chaos, Goldberg and Horwood point to "Exhibit A," the City of Houston - which has never enacted such legislation in its entire history:

> "The very existence of a large North American city (an area in excess of five hundred square miles and a population of 1.6 million) which can function normally and continue to grow without zoning is a major piece of evidence against the traditional view that zoning supposedly protects against chaos."

Divergent tastes

Our authors painstakingly survey several empirical land use studies in Pittsburgh, Boston, Rochester, Houston, and Vancouver, which trace the effects of "incompatible uses" on property values. They report that the overwhelming preponderance of evidence "cast(s) serious doubt upon...the presence of uniform external diseconomies."[†] The reality appears to be that either there are few significant interdependencies and externalities in urban property markets or that "One man's meat is another man's poison." One and the same phenome-

---

† Editor's Note: External diseconomies are said to prevail when A harms B by doing C, and B cannot collect damages nor force A to cease and desist from such activities. Uniformity would mean that all market participants view C as harmful.

non, such as the presence of commerce in an otherwise residential neighborhood, is interpreted in a positive way by some people and in a negative way by others.

The market process

Goldberg and Horwood forcefully maintain "that market mechanisms exist naturally to eliminate such externalities that would arise from the proverbial glue factory on the corner of Portage and Main." In a system based on the inviolability of private property rights, the laws of nuisance would prevent the dispersion of invasive odors, or dust particles. But the market mechanism functions even without this protection. Quite simply, land prices in the residential or business neighborhoods are too expensive for the glue factory; they effectively prohibit any but the most valuable, concentrated uses - such as large office buildings or high rise residential dwellings.

This view is supported by Roscoe H. Jones, Houston's Director of City Planning, and author of an appendix to the Fraser Institute zoning study: (The market) "has tended to create a reasonably well-ordered pattern. Because of private 'marketplace zoning,' we find no filling stations at the end of cul-de-sacs; ship channel industries are, naturally, located along the Ship Channel, and so on."

Urban density

The natural proclivities of the market can also be utilized to banish the spectre of the "hit and run" land developer who is said to leave an excessive population in his wake, swamping municipal services.

A developer who tried to pack too many people into an office building would have difficulty finding mortgage assistance. Lenders would realize that such compressed conditions would overload services, resulting in tenant dissatisfaction, lower rents, and the possibility of mortgage default. It is of course true that builders and lenders can make mistakes, and that some overcrowded structures might be built, but the inexorable forces of profit and loss would ensure that such errors were few in number. Zoners are likewise subject to miscalculation; the problem is that there are no automatic bankruptcy procedures to weed out bureaucrats with poor judgement. Say Goldberg and Horwood in this regard, "One of the most persuasive arguments against zoning is the fact that it institutionalizes errors...In effect, planners do not have the incentives to 'get it right,' nor do they suffer the consequences of 'getting it wrong'." The competitive system thus can obviate the need for building height restrictions, set back requirements, floor space ratios, and other bureaucratic measures which artificially attempt to limit density.

Undue strain on public services

The typical pro zoning argument is couched not in terms of undue strain on halls and elevators, which are internal to the building, but rather in terms of the effects of high density on social overhead capital: electricity, gas, water, sewers, roads, sidewalks, parking, public transit, parks - all of which are external to the subject premises; i.e., externalities.

But this should give us pause for thought. For surely there are other amenities necessary for the successful functioning of a large office building, which are or can be considered externalities, but which do not concern the city planner nor unduly worry anyone else: for example, restaurants, barber shops, banks, jewelry stores, pharmacies, stationers, etc. One reason may be that every member of the former category is run by public or quasi-public enterprises while the latter are all managed privately.

When the excavation for a new office building is begun, the small merchants in the neighborhood roll up their sleeves in gleeful anticipation of the new customers and additional profits likely to come their way. Their first thoughts are concerned with physical expansion, adding extra shifts, providing more services. The contrast with the bureaucratic orientation is stark indeed. At the prospect of new building, their tendency is to ponder the "strain" additional hordes of people will place on public services. Their answer is to place a myriad of zoning restrictions on the new builders instead of encouraging coordinated expansion.

Thus it appears that if error and hence the need for correction lies anywhere, it is not with the "rapacious builder" who places "strains" on public services, but rather with those charged with the provision of the infrastructure: those in the government sector. Perhaps the answer lies in improving the provision of these services, not in holding down new construction.

A useful comparison is the case of Houston. Here the practice is not to hem in the private market with a bewildering array of complex zoning restrictions, but rather to *cooperate* with the land developer by "forecast(ing) the growth patterns in order that the city government may supply the necessary municipal facilities and services at the right time, at the right size, and at the right place." The authors of this monograph emphasize the point that zoning is only one weapon in the planning arsenal: even were these restrictions scrapped in their entirety, the public authorities would still exercise great control over land use patterns through (1) provision of infrastructure and amenities, such as parks, water mains, sewer placements, and the layout of freeway and major arterial streets; and (2) direct land use controls concerning building heights, set backs, floor space ratios, etc., but applied uniformly to an entire city, and not differentially to districts within its boundaries. This does indeed undercut much of the case for zoning. But in the interest of creating further discussion, one might even question whether government has a comparative advantage, vis-à-vis the market, in the creation of such products and controls. The public official, after all, has no communication from the deity indicating the optimal location for a park or sewer line. Without a market-created price system, it is extremely difficult for him to rationally allocate resources. Moreover, no profit or loss automatically accrues to him as a spur in decision making. He risks none of his own money, and can earn no honest profit from correct choices.

Declining property values

There are few things feared more by the average urban property owner than declining residential values. This is understandable, for much of the real savings of the typical citizen is tied up in a single family house. Perhaps this is the single most important explanation for the high regard with which many citizens hold zoning legislation - it is supposed to protect property values.

But the view that zoning is the best guarantee of stability is inconsistent with the evidence: "The stability of neighborhoods that zoning seeks to protect thus appears to be endangered by the rezoning that is part and parcel of the enactment of zoning by-laws in the first place." What security can zoning provide against the possible ravages of the glue factory if its provisions can be rescinded at any time?

Of far greater reliability may be the system of deed restrictions, or restrictive covenants, as practiced in Houston, whereby the property owner may contract with his neighbors concerning the uses to which land may subsequently be put. Alternatively, land developers may require, as a condition of sale, that all purchasers agree to continued land usage, either for a stipulated (long) period of time or until a majority vote of such buyers overturns the agreement.

This system is far more flexible. Even "the maintenance of single family neighborhoods by zoning statutes," state Goldberg and Horwood, "is...questionable: by keeping land and buildings in the same use over time, zoning can promote neighborhood decay and speed the demise of the single family neighborhood. Zoning is a rigid control, and is likely to fracture during times of change in consumer tastes, neighborhood demographic structure, urban growth, and transportation and building technologies."

Ultimately, of course, there can be no absolute guarantee against declining property values. A fall in the price of wood, an increase in the market rate of interest, the sale of Crown lands, technological improvements in prefabrication methods can all lower housing prices. One might perhaps contract with an insurance company for the preservation of home values, but the cost of the premium payments would have to be subtracted, thus defeating the plan.

Value preservation is a will o' the wisp, for price is a manifestation of the worth placed on an item not by one person, but by two groups: potential sellers and potential buyers of items like the one in question. Not only can we not speak with certainty of the value an owner will place on his home in the future; it is even less possible to assess the worth a future hypothetical buyer will give it. It is clear, moreover, that that which is owned is the physical house, and not its value. For while the owner has a right to collect damages from the boy who breaks a window with a ball, he has no such right with respect to the man who invented prefabricated housing - even though the latter might well have been responsible for a greater drop in the value of his house than the former.

While citizens have a clear and obvious right to have their homes protected from physical damage, this does not apply to the *value* of their property. Yet this is precisely what zoning seeks to preserve. Thus not only must such legislation fail to accomplish this task - it would be improper even if it could do so.

Uniformity

Another shortcoming associated with zoning is the uniformity it engenders. And this is not surprising: to divide all building into residential, commercial, and industrial, as the early enactments did, and then to impose these three categories upon the entire pattern of future construction, is hardly likely to foster architectural innovation.

This rigidity soon became evident, and an effort was made to become more "flexible." The zoning codes added variances, exceptions, Planned Unit Developments (PUDs) (any excess building in one parcel is to be offset by a reduction in another within the planning district), mixed-use zones, performance zoning systems, land use contracts, and development permits. In one respect these reforms were a plus, for the system became less rigid. But this change ushered in a new crop of problems. For one thing, the system became even more complex. Literally dozens of districts have been defined; what may and may not be done with each is subject to a bewildering and growing number of regulations. Say Goldberg and Horwood, "The days of three district zoning with two or three pages of regulations have long since passed. Today's ordinances are continually growing to accommodate more detailed regulations of use, lot size, building height and bulk; more reasons for granting variances, bonuses, and special exceptions; and much more complicated procedures for appeals and reviews." Things have come to such a pass that no self-respecting set of zoning regulations dare appear in a tome of less than 500 pages.

For another, a system with so many complications, exceptions and changes could no longer be governed by any clear set of rules or principles. The procedure instead became one of "judging each case on its merits" in an ad hoc manner.

Although this might appear to some as fair and judicious, the flaws in it are grave. First, it is a clear retreat from the idea of zoning itself. According to this philosophy, urban planners were assumed to have enough wisdom to forecast, at least in broad brush strokes, the future spatial organization of the city. But the very need to grant numerous exceptions, as a continuing institutionalized process, has belied this claim. Ability to incorporate the needs of a changing future is simply incompatible with patchwork changes as reality confronts the master plan. It is akin to claiming the ability to forecast inflation for the next five years - and then changing the prognostication each week.

The rule of law

Secondly, as Nobel Laureates Milton Friedman and Friedrich

Hayek have so eloquently shown, "judging each case on its merits" is the *absence* of lawfulness - not its presence. Each has demonstrated (the former in his analysis of "rules not authorities" in monetary policy; the latter in his work on the "rule of law") that to consider matters on a "case by case" basis is to color the judicial process with stultifying arbitrariness.

The proper scope of government, in this view, is to set down the rules of the game, clearly, and before the contest begins - and then not to continually alter them in the midst of the fray. Under these conditions, the individual is free to pursue his lawful ends, secure in the reasonable knowledge that the government powers will not suddenly be used to frustrate him at every turn. But a zoning system, especially a "flexible" or "reformed" one, can change the uses to which a land parcel may be put at any time. It is thus clearly destructive of these ends.

Graft

Thirdly, zoning complexity and changeability have spawned graft and corruption. The reason for this is easy to discern: a less restrictive variance may be worth millions of dollars to the land developer. Be the bureaucrat ever so honest, he will be sorely tempted by a share in these gains - especially in an era where rezoning is an easily contrived and commonplace occurrence. Paradoxically, this is not necessarily all to the bad. If a bribe can convert a land parcel to a use more highly prized by consumers, wealth and the allocation of resources will have been much more nearly optimized. This is not the first case on record attesting to the benefits of black markets. The great loss, however, is the general disrespect for the law engendered by this practice.

Private zoning

If zoning can be defined as matching specific areas of land with particular uses, then nothing said above should be interpreted as opposing *private* zoning. Indeed, it is impossible for any rational land developer to act in any other way. He must, if he is to function at all, decide to place the garage here, the house there, and the backyard elsewhere. How else could he conceivably operate? But this is all that is meant by private zoning.

The case is an exact parallel to the planning debate. As has been said many times before, people must plan if they are to act rationally. The debate, then, is not between planning and non-planning. It is between central planning, on the part of the government, and individual planning, as coordinated through the marketplace. Similarly the real issue here is not the choice between zoning and non-zoning; it is between private and governmental zoning. What has been criticized above is *government* zoning, not the private variety.

What is private zoning? The most well-known example is, of course, Houston's system of deed restrictions. Private zoning also takes place every time a glue factory is priced out of a residential neighborhood, or whenever the gas station locates on a major thoroughfare, not in a side street. But it also includes such prosaic activities as the individual's arrangement of household furniture, the office's placement of desks and room dividers, the factory's disposition of machines and guardrails, and the shopping mall's apportionment of its tenants.

Items for sale must be deployed in the most advantageous manner possible. Thus merchants match store areas to particular uses. The success of each enterprise rests, in great part, upon the skill in such "zoning." If the grocer discovers, for example, that apples and oranges sell better in close proximity, or that the juxtaposition of corn and peas detracts from the sale of both, without any offsetting benefits on the remainder of the stock, he can profit by incorporating this information into his "zoning" decision making. He will gain a competitive advantage over those of his colleagues who are not similarly skilled. It is in this way that the market promotes efficient zoning.

The same process is at work in shopping centers and malls. Since the various tenants are contractually unrelated to one another, the situation is closely analogous to governmental zoning. Private entrepreneurs, however, are judged, in their profit and loss accounts, by how well they promote positive externalities and repress negative ones. And, in fact, it is difficult to imagine two "incompatible" tenants adjacent to each other in a shopping mall. Any inclination toward such mal-zoning tends to be rigidly suppressed by the market.

There is a vast reservoir of private zoning efforts operating in the economy, unreported, under-publicized. This brief discussion has barely scratched the surface. But it can be viewed as an adjunct to Goldberg and Horwood's excellent critique of public zoning efforts.

What are the public policy recommendations of this study? Although the authors are cautious and offer no explicit panaceas, they do favor movements toward the non-zoning extreme. Goldberg and Horwood conclude: "Zoning has not worked very well. The externalities that it is designed to ameliorate have been shown to be minimal or non-existent...The maintenance of single family neighborhoods by zoning statutes is also questionable..."

The Fraser Institute is pleased to publish *Zoning: Its Costs and Relevance for the 1980s* in the interests of promoting public discussion of this important public policy area. However, owing to the independence of its authors, the views expressed may or may not conform severally or collectively with those of the members of the Institute.

January 1980   **Walter Block**

About the Authors

David E. Baxter is President of Daedalus Investments Incorporated, Vancouver, British Columbia. Previously he was Assistant Professor in the Urban Land Economics Division of the Faculty of Commerce and Business Administration at the University of British Columbia. He has taught courses in Land Economics, Real Estate Finance, and Public Land Policy. Born in 1945, Mr. Baxter carried out his undergraduate studies at the University of Alberta and his graduate studies at the University of British Columbia. He has served as a consultant in the fields of housing, land use and land development policy, analysis of regional economic structure, regional employment and land use forecasting, and evaluation of community planning documents.

Among his publications are: *Landlords and Tenants in Danger - Rent Control in Canada* (with S.W. Hamilton), published by the Appraisal Institute of Canada in 1975; *Capital Taxes Pertaining to Real Property* (with S.W. Hamilton), published by the Real Estate Institute of British Columbia in 1975; "Market Effects of Legislation Controlling Foreign Investment," in P. Horwood (ed.) *Foreign Investment in Land*

- *Alternative Controls*, published by the University of British Columbia in 1976; and "Government Ownership and the Price of Land" (with S.W. Hamilton), which appeared in *Public Property? The Habitat Debate Continued...*, Lawrence B. Smith and Michael Walker (eds.), published by the Fraser Institute in 1977.

Walter Block is Senior Economist at the Fraser Institute and a member of the Economics Department at Rutgers University. Born in Brooklyn, New York, in 1941, Dr. Block received his B.A. from Brooklyn College in 1964 and his Ph.D. from Columbia University in 1972. He has taught Microeconomics, Industrial Organization, Urban Economics, and Political Economy at Stony Brook, State University of New York; the City College of New York, New York University; and Baruch College, City University of New York; and has worked in various research capacities for the National Bureau of Economic Research, the Tax Foundation, and *Business Week* Magazine.

Professor Block has published numerous articles on economic theory in *Growth & Change, Theory & Decision, The American Economist, The Journal of Libertarian Studies, Real Estate Quarterly,* and *Reason.* A former Cato Institute Fellow, Earhart Fellow, and New York State Regents Fellowship winner, he is the author of *Defending the Undefendable,* published by Fleet Press, New York, in 1976.

Michael A. Goldberg is Visiting Scholar (1979/80), Harvard University and a Professor in the Urban Land Economics Division, Faculty of Commerce and Business Administration, at the University of British Columbia. Born in Brooklyn, New York, in 1941, Professor Goldberg received his B.A. in Economics (cum laude) from Brooklyn College in 1962. His post-graduate work was done at the University of California (Berkeley), where he received his M.A. degree in 1965 and his Ph.D. in Economics in 1968. He joined the University of British Columbia in 1968.

Professor Goldberg is author of numerous books and articles that have been published in Canada, the United States, and Japan. His recent publications include: "Residential Developer Behaviour 1975: A Detailed Analysis and Findings" (with D.D. Ulinder), in *Housing: It's Your Move* (Vancouver: Urban Land Economics Division, Faculty of Commerce and Business Administration, University of British

Columbia, 1976); *Recent Perspectives in Urban Land Economics: Essays in Honour of Richard U. Ratcliff and Paul F. Wendt* (ed.), (Vancouver: Urban Land Economics Division, Faculty of Commerce and Business Administration, University of British Columbia, 1976); and "Simulating Cities: Process, Product and Prognosis," *Journal of the American Institute of Planners* (1977). Professor Goldberg was a contributor to *Urban Housing Markets: Recent Directions in Research and Policy*, Larry S. Bourne and John R. Hitchcock (eds.), published by the University of Toronto Press, 1978. Two of his papers have appeared in earlier Fraser Institute publications: "Housing and Land Prices in Canada and the U.S." in *Public Property? The Habitat Debate Continued...*, Lawrence B. Smith and Michael Walker (eds.), 1977; and "The BNA Act, NHA, CMHC, MSUA, etc.: 'Nymophobia' and the On-going Search for an Appropriate Canadian Housing & Urban Development Policy," in *Canadian Confederation at the Crossroads: The Search for a Federal-Provincial Balance*, Michael Walker (ed.), 1978.

Peter J. Horwood is a freelance consultant in the urban land economics field engaged in work for both the public and private sectors. His graduate studies concentrated on urban housing market research. He received his B.A. and M.Sc. (Bus.Admin.) degrees in Urban Land Economics from the University of British Columbia.

His previous publications examined foreign investment in land, the factors affecting housing demand, and the residential conveyance process in Canada. Mr. Horwood was a member of the University Endowment Lands Study Team and the Greenspan Task Force on Residential Land, and editor of *Foreign Investment in Land - Alternative Controls*, published by the University of British Columbia in 1976.

Roscoe H. Jones was born in Vinita, Oklahoma, in 1925. He graduated from Oklahoma State University in 1947 with a B.Sc. in Civil Engineering with distinction and received his Master of City Planning degree from the Harvard University Graduate School of Design in 1950.

After serving as a city planner in the cities of Tulsa, Oklahoma; Oklahoma City, Oklahoma; Cambridge, Massachusetts; and Miami, Florida, Mr. Jones served as Director of Planning and Engineering for Ottumwa, Iowa; Director of Planning and Traffic in Springfield, Missouri; and Director of

Planning for Metropolitan Dade County in Miami, Florida. He was appointed to his present position of Director of City Planning for the City of Houston in 1964.

Mr. Jones taught City Planning at the University of Miami, Dade County Community College, Houston Baptist University, and was Associate Professor of City Planning at the University of Houston from 1964 to 1968.

CHAPTER ONE
Introduction, Purpose, and Overview

CHAPTER ONE
Introduction, Purpose, and Overview

In the year 1916, an act of the New York State legislature delegated authority to the City of New York to enact the first comprehensive zoning ordinance in North America. In essence, this gave the city authority to designate certain areas for specific land uses through the creation of "residential zones," "industrial zones," etc. From the first rumor of this foray by local government into the area of land use control to the present day, zoning has provided a platform for some of the most lively and emotional debates regarding the use of our urban environment.

After more than sixty years of zoning, enthusiasm for the topic does not seem to have dampened. Anyone doubting the validity of this statement has merely to sit in at a board of variance hearing, convened to pass judgement on a request to alter the zoning status of a particular parcel of land. Regardless of whether the change involves a move from single family to multiple, industrial to commercial, or whether the hearing takes place in Halifax or Moose Jaw, the casual observer will witness arguments ranging from economics to mental health, presented in anything from elaborate audio-visual displays to simple hand wringing, tears, and cursing.

The reason for the emotional nature of today's debates results essentially from the same fear of declining property values that inspired the Fifth Avenue merchants in New York City to demand protection for their fashionable stores some sixty years ago. Obviously, a perceived threat to an individual's investment will always generate a heated response. When real property is at stake, the aura of "a man's castle" adds a special fire to the debate, regardless of whether the investment is being protected or impeded by zoning. With this special interest, it is not surprising that zoning occupies a very prominent position of interest and concern.

Given its widespread adoption throughout North America, and its place of prominence in the public eye, it is surprising that zoning has not received more attention from empirical researchers. The paucity of such material is due in part to our inherent faith/belief in the necessity of zoning as a protection from the chaos of urban growth.

> Zoning is the first fundamental step in any city to establish a practical basis for constructive city growth. Until zoning is done, no city planning is done, no city planning commission can effectively prove its case as to the necessity for the adoption of a major street plan, or properly promote greater economy, convenience, safety, health and comfort in industrial, business or living conditions; or make the city more beautiful and attractive.[1]

We have always accepted the "first fundamental step." Our debates have occurred within the framework of the zoning philosophy: "whether parcel 'A' should be rezoned to commercial" or "whether such variants as mixed use zones are as equitable as simple zoning."

The central theme of this book is to move back to the first step and ask the question posed by opponents of such legislation in 1916: "Is zoning necessary?" As trite as this may sound, the answer is far from obvious.

The purpose behind this question is to present an economic view of zoning. The material contained here can provide an understanding of the nature and diversity of the zoning ordinance through its sixty-plus years of development. A central part of the analysis will be a review of the conceptual and empirical evidence to date. In addition, the history and the rationales given for zoning will be presented, to allow the reader to assess the effectiveness and the need for this ordinance.

Chapter two presents a general history of zoning and its development into a variety of forms. Although the North American strain is over sixty years old, European experience has existed since 1884. It is generally agreed that enactments in the German cities of Altona and Frankfurt-am-Main, complete with ordinances that specified building height and set backs, were the forerunners of the present system.[2] However, modern zoning ordinances are the result of considerable development over the years. Prefixes such as exclusionary, fiscal, mixed-use, and performance have been added to the traditional instrument in response to changing demands on the function of zoning. Its complexity has been greatly increased by the addition of sections, sub-sections, bonuses, exemptions, and variances. One indication of this is the fact that it is now impossible for any city to distribute its code without a charge to cover the extended printing costs.

It is not surprising that complexity is one of the central complaints against present-day zoning. In chapter three, the pros and cons of the debate are examined, focusing on the accusations of inflexibility, socio-economic exclusion, and the kind of intricateness that led one city planner to complain "that only the city attorney and he understood the zoning ordinance."[3] On the other side of the coin, a large number of planners maintain that zoning is essential in the reduction of land use conflicts. Furthermore, they believe in many instances that this policy helps to protect areas of the city which have a special character, allows the public authority to provide better public facilities, and shifts some of those costs to the developers of new residential property.

There is a further aspect which will be examined in this chapter - the contention that zoning has outlived its usefulness. This argument suggests that zoning has, within reason, accomplished everything it set out to do in New York, circa 1916. However, it is claimed, times have changed and the demands placed on our land use controls today cannot be met by the traditional zoning ordinance. As one reporter expressed it, "zoning may be the land use dinosaur of the 70's."[4]

The majority of the empirical evidence to date has been established in U.S. studies that attempt to measure the side effects of zoning. As one researcher noted:

> The best evidence (of zoning's side effects) would come from comparing a map of land use in a zoned city with a similar (hypothetical) map of the same city unzoned. Such a comparison would tell us precisely the modifications due to zoning regulations in both the quantity and the geographic specialization of land in various uses. But the existence of one map precludes the existence of the other...we must approach the question...by seeking evidence on whether zoning has observable side effects.[5]

A synopsis of the published empirical evidence is presented in chapter four. The central theme of the U.S. methodology has been to express the transaction price of residential property as a function of a number of variables which were originally identified by Brigham.[6] In Brigham's work, these variables included such characteristics as accessibility to the urban core, the topography and amenities of the site. The effect of the surrounding area on property values, which to a certain extent zoning seeks to control, is viewed as part of the amenities variable. The methodology attempts to hold all things constant other than those amenity factors associated with zoning. In this manner, the effect of the zoning variable on the price of the property may be isolated and measured.

Following this methodology, researchers have studied the effect of externalities and the allocation of land use within an urban market: the two mainstay arguments supporting zoning. Negative externalities, such as the sights and smells of a glue factory as viewed on neighboring residential property, are the traditional justification for zoning. Proponents state that land use must be controlled or property values stand to be adversely affected. More recently, zoning has also been viewed as a device to ensure that the proportionate division of land uses is established for the "public good" rather than the "narrow goal" of market efficiency.

Unfortunately there has not been sufficient research from which to draw categorical conclusions. However, these studies have raised questions about the good effects of zoning and its necessity, which for years have been taken for granted.

In Roscoe Jones' appendix to this chapter, he examines the City of Houston and its unique position of development without zoning. With a population of well over a million and an area in excess of five hundred square miles, the very existence of Houston casts doubt upon the necessity of zoning as a protector against urban chaos.

Chapter five of this book presents an empirical examination of zoning in a Canadian milieu. This material is a synthesis of two studies conducted in the Vancouver area. The data are used to investigate the effect of zoning on speculative transactions within the residential property market and the effect that rezoning has on property values within the rezoned area and on adjoining parcels. As with the American studies, the results are in conflict with the traditional views of zoning.

In chapter six, the issues outlined earlier are reviewed in light of the evidence presented. The implications for current zoning practices are analyzed and reforms suggested. In addition, various alternatives to the system of zoning as a whole are discussed.

Finally, in the appendix to the book, David Baxter provides a graphical analysis of the effects of land use controls on the urban land market. The material presents an economic model of land use markets, displaying the spatial distribution of rents and uses. After the basic model is established, the analysis proceeds to show the effect of the introduction of zoning and compares market operation in its presence and absence. The model is extended to display the effects on expectations and market operations, given the possibility of changes in the status of zoning.

Notes

Any undertaking such as this requires the assistance of a number of people. Mark Ricketts provided the initial push needed to launch the project, as well as assistance on the first draft. Jim Cameron assisted in the preparation of the tables in chapter five on the rezoning in Vancouver. Alice AuCoin, Ruth Calder, and Sally Pipes copy-edited the manuscript. Laurie Hustler assisted in the design of the illustrations in the appendix and Ruth Calder compiled the bibliography. Despite the efforts made on our behalf by the foregoing individuals, errors doubtless still remain, for which we assume full responsibility.

1 C. Cheney, "Removing Social Barriers by Zoning," p. 276.

2 Harold M. Lewis, *Planning the Modern City*, pp. 256-257.

3 See appendix to chapter four.

4 Neal R. Pierce, "Will Zoning be the Dinosaur of the '70's?," p. 5A.

5 Steven M. Maser et al., "The Effects of Zoning and Externalities on the Price of Land," p. 113.

6 Eugene F. Brigham, "The Determinants of Residential Land Values," p. 325.

CHAPTER TWO
History and Diversity

CHAPTER TWO
History and Diversity

I. SOME HISTORY

North American development

To provide a background for our discussion of zoning, this chapter begins with a brief history of the development of the ordinance in North America. In the second part of the chapter the basic zoning device will be outlined and then a number of recent variations currently in use will be discussed.

Prior to New York's legislative action in 1916, land use control in North America had been limited for the most part to private actions related to the laws of nuisance or restrictive covenants. The only departures were discriminatory laws phrased in land use terms, but obviously aimed at segregating Chinese workers or the native population.

> ...(it is) unlawful for any person to establish, maintain, or carry on the business of a public laundry...within the city of Modesto, except that part of the city which lies west of the railroad track and south of G street....
>
> (Modesto, California - 1885)[1]

11

At approximately the same time as such exclusionary ordinances were operating in California, New York was suffering from the growing pains of a burgeoning garment industry encroaching on the high society of Fifth Avenue.

> Nothing so blasting to the best class of business and property interests has ever been seen or known in any great retail district in any large city as this vast flood of workers which sweeps down the pavements at noontime every day and literally overwhelms and engulfs shops, shopkeepers and the shopping public.[2]

This problem, coupled with the so-called skyscraper developments of the twentieth century, led to the formation of the New York Advisory Commission on the Height of Buildings in 1913. The Commission's report is generally agreed to be "the beginning of the zoning movement in America."[3] By 1916 New York had established land use districts which stipulated height, area, and use limitations. The New York zoning by-law gained great popularity, and the federal government in 1926 passed the *Standard Zoning Enabling Act*, which had been adopted in twenty-nine states by 1930. Even before this was passed, the appeal of the ordinance had motivated eighty-five cities and towns in twenty-one states to adopt a city-wide zoning plan by 1922.[4]

European evolution

At the same time that New York City zoning was being held up for public accolade, regulation of urban land use through zoning was coming into effect in Germany. Europeans had long accepted the notion that regulation of land use was necessary to promote sanitary conditions and the aesthetic appeal of their cities. Ordinances stipulating zones for use, building height, and set backs were in operation in Altona and Frankfurt-am-Main by 1891. By 1912 the degree of acceptance of zoning had reached the point where the City of Karlsruhe had an ordinance containing sixteen classes of streets.[5] These advances in urban land use control, when viewed along with the prosperity and development of German cities in general, were quickly hailed as the saviour of modern urban planning.

The British development of land use controls was quite different, stemming largely from the philosophical base upon which real property rights rest. In America, property rights have achieved a far more sanctified place than in the United Kingdom. U.S. land use controls grew out of the idea that the individual has a right to develop his own property to its highest and best use and be protected from harmful development of other property owners. The right to develop is one of the rights of ownership. Property rights under the British Common Law have evolved differently into a body of enactments called Development Control. "Development Control essentially requires that all use change and development of land in England, Wales and Scotland proceed only by way of permission from local government sources. There is no inherent right to develop land in whatever fashion the owner might wish, and each application for permission to develop land or change its use is regarded on its own individual merits."[6]

The first legislation was passed in 1909. The *Housing, Town Planning Act* gave local governments the right to create plans for, and regulate development of, areas likely to be built upon in the future. In 1932, legislation enabled similar control of previously built-up areas as well as land not likely to be developed. The present legislation, passed in 1968, builds upon the 1947 *Town and Country Planning Act* which was largely based on the *Final Report by the Expert Committee on Compensation and Betterment, 1942*, also known by the name of its chairman, Mr. Justice Uthwatt. The *Uthwatt Report* revolved around the philosophy that land ownership represents duties to the community as well as rights of development to the owner. The idea that was to grow out of this was the right of the public (e.g., the Crown) to take from the owner any increment in land value resulting from development permission at higher uses. But the regulation of development became encumbered in bureaucratic entanglements. This led to the present decentralized legislation which relies on the creation of a *local plan* which depends upon the prior establishment of a broad set of development guidelines called a *structural plan*. It is important to note that the philosophy of the *Uthwatt Report* still looms large in British land use control and that, in contrast with the U.S., a great deal more authority rests in the hands of local administrative bodies. U.S. legislation has from the beginning shied away from administrative control of property and other rights, placing more responsibility upon elected officials, be they local councils, judges, or local special purpose boards. The broad administrative discretion exercised in Britain is virtually unknown in the U.S. Land use control is much more highly politicized in the United States than in either the United Kingdom or Canada.

Canadian tradition - private owners are trustees for the Crown

Canadian land use control has closely followed the U.S. practice until recently by relying heavily on the use of zoning by-laws to control development. But this similarity is really quite superficial and results from the resemblance of the legislation in the two countries and from the historical evolution of their respective cities. Underlying these like-nesses are deep-seated differences in the constitutions and legal systems. In Canada, there is much greater adminis-trative discretion than in the U.S., and notions of private property, though strongly rooted, do not dominate. The property owner is still a trustee for the Crown and has rights bestowed by the Crown, which is almost the opposite of the U.S. practice.

Canadian land use controls began at the turn of the century with minimal building regulations governing frontage and set backs, along with some discretionary power to regulate use. "Districting" analogous to New York zoning was implemented in Ontario in 1921. This was followed one year later with the passage of a zoning by-law in the municipality of Point Grey, British Columbia. This by-law was extended to the City of Vancouver in 1927 when the two cities merged.

In general, most provinces adopted land use controls similar to the U.S. model, with significant innovations being brought into law after 1950. Alberta created development control legislation modelled after the 1947 *Town and Country Planning Act* in the United Kingdom. Other provinces have followed this example, while seven at the present time have enacted both traditional zoning and more flexible develop-ment controls.

II. THE CHARACTER OF ZONING BY-LAWS

Originally intended as "police powers"

When zoning was originally introduced, it was promoted under the auspices of the so-called "police powers." These called for the protection of the health, safety, convenience, and welfare of the public. Although the majority of today's ordinances still make direct reference to the protection of these four items in relation to the act of zoning, the basic document has undergone a process of significant enlargement and variation.

Current practice - segregating land use

The standard municipal zoning ordinance begins with a map displaying the division of the municipality into districts. For each of these districts the ordinance presents regulations governing the use of buildings or land, the height and bulk of structures, the lot dimensions, and open space requirements.

In the definition of building and land use, the number of categories involved will always be at least three: residential, commercial, and industrial. However, with the desire of local authorities to govern all uses, provision for at least twenty sub-categories or more is not unusual. These uses are usually related on a hierarchic scale, with use of single family dwellings traditionally occupying the highest classification. Single family units are not considered to be a source of negative externalities (diseconomies) to any other uses, whereas all "lower order" uses are viewed as such for higher uses on the scale. Hence, higher and lower uses ideally should be separated. Earlier ordinances did allow "higher order" uses to occur in lower districts; however, later planning theory has suggested that total separation of uses may be more beneficial to the public good.

Height and bulk regulation - the livability objective

In regulating the height and bulk of structures, the specifications of the zoning ordinance are "aimed directly at the qualities that collectively contribute to 'livability'."[7]   A typical device of this category of regulation is the limitation of the floor space ratio (fsr). This ratio specifies the relationship between the floor area of the structure and the area of the lot on which it is placed. For example, an fsr of 2.0 on a 60,000 square foot lot would allow for a structure offering 120,000 square feet of usable space. The fsr does not by itself regulate the height of the structure. There is usually a maximum height specified by the ordinance in terms of either a number of stories or a number of feet. Both the fsr and the height regulations are involved in the device of "bonusing" or "premiums." By allowing for an increase in the fsr or the height, the ordinance creates economic leverage by permitting the construction of more rentable area in return for the provision of certain public benefits (e.g., plazas, set backs, etc.). A further aspect of this type of regulation is the "bulk control plane," an effort to control a building's interference with the light and air of neighboring structures.

Regulations regarding lot dimensions and open space requirements also contribute to the "livability" ideal inherent in the zoning ordinance. The lot area itself can directly affect the population density of an area by requiring a minimum lot size for each dwelling unit. Yard regulations work with the lot area to specify minimum front and rear yard dimensions and minimum set backs from the property line. In essence, these regulations dictate how a structure may sit on its lot. Diagonally sitting structures, for example, are traditionally contrary to the zoning ordinance. In addition to these requirements, in multiple family residential, commercial, and industrial zones, this category of regulation is used to specify certain amounts of open space to be provided per unit or structure, and to specify the number of off-street parking stalls to be provided per unit.

Some token participatory democracy

The zoning ordinance also provides for public input. Regulations for establishing boards of review, procedures for appealing to the board for exceptions to the present zoning, and the granting of variances or requests for bonusing are all contained in the ordinance. The inclusion of a quasi-judicial review body was added with the purpose of imparting a degree of flexibility and humanity to the ordinance. The board usually allows for exceptions in situations involving unreasonable "hardship" for a property owner resulting from strict enforcement of the ordinance. In addition, these boards rule on those cases that cannot be conveniently placed in any particular category.

This brief description of the standard zoning ordinance has only touched on the major provisions. The days of three district zoning with two or three pages of regulations have long since passed. Today's ordinances are continually growing to accommodate more detailed regulations of use, lot size, building height, and bulk; more reasons for granting variances, bonuses, and special exceptions; and much more complicated procedures for appeals and reviews.

III. VARIATIONS ON THE ZONING THEME

In addition to the increasing complexity of the standard ordinance, recent years have seen the development of a number of variations of the basic instrument. The "need" for these variants stems in some cases from an adjustment of the basic goal, but more often it results from changing urban land use demands that could not be accommodated by the standard document.

Mixed-use zoning

The principal area requiring accommodation was the absolute separation of uses. The basic law was typically far too rigid to allow compatible uses that were not of the same type, even where large area subdivisions were involved. Hence, the establishment of a neighborhood grocery store in a new residential development was impossible. To correct this, Mixed-Use Zones (MXDs) were devised to allow for certain compatible uses. But this did not represent a move to total flexibility. The standard regulations of height, bulk, lot size, etc., were still in effect and further regulations were added to specify what mixtures were allowed and in what proportions. MXDs dot the Canadian central city landscape in Halifax, Montreal, Toronto, Edmonton, Calgary, and Vancouver.

Planned Unit Developments

Planned Unit Developments (PUDs) typically follow these mixed-use zones. As with their predecessor, they were developed to cope with the inflexibility of the ordinance. However, in the case of PUDs, this related to the regulations of height, bulk, and density of the individual lot rather than use for a specific area. In general, PUDs must conform to the established regulations, but their performance is viewed over the entire development rather than on a lot-by-lot basis. Thus, if an *fsr* of 2.0 is required by the zoning by-law, PUDs must adhere to this for the project in total; however, this may include certain individual lots having an *fsr* of 6.0. In essence, the incorporation of PUDs shifts the regulations from a lot basis to a project basis. Pioneered in the United States, PUDs have found favor in Ontario, the Maritimes, and Alberta as innovative means for developing urban land.

Performance zoning

Performance zoning moves a step beyond mixed-use zoning by specifying the functions that must be performed in the zone (e.g., housing, retail, and personal services) without tying the

17

development to specific design and intensity guidelines. As with PUDs and MXDs, performance zoning is most advantageously applied to larger projects which can accommodate mixes of uses and intensities.

Land use contracts

The ultimate in flexible zoning is a variant known as land use contracts, which until quite recently operated in Alberta and British Columbia.[8]   This particular device made all land use completely negotiable within certain designated areas of the municipality. With the unlimited scope of a legal contract, everything required by either party could be specified in the greatest of detail, thus making the zoning specific to a particular development proposal rather than an area of land.

Exclusionary and fiscal zoning

Exclusionary and fiscal zoning are two further variants of the standard ordinance. However, these forms have resulted in adjusting the goal from one of urban order and property protection, to that of excluding unwanted uses. Fiscal zoning involves a manipulation of the regulations to produce a net tax receipt gain by excluding consumers of large amounts of public services and attracting those uses which can contribute relatively larger amounts of property tax revenue.

> Favored under this system are light industry, research and development firms and, to a lesser degree, low density residential zones with high value, single-family homes. Multi-family units, mobile homes and higher density homes are commonly prohibited uses.[9]

The term exclusionary zoning is used when the manipulation of the regulations is backed by discriminatory motives. The adjustment of the regulations are devised to specifically exclude certain socio-economic groups.

> A locality may effect prohibitive minimum price levels for new residential development by zoning its undeveloped lands for predominantly single-family homes with requirements for large lots, large frontages, and large livable floor areas to the exclusion of multi-family units and mobile homes. The impact of such zoning policies falls most heavily upon racial minorities since their

ranks are proportionately greater than whites among low and moderate income households.[10]

In essence, this form of zoning is a return to the 1885 ordinance of the City of Modesto referred to earlier. Unfortunately, such discrimination is easy to disguise in the form of fiscal zoning.

Diversity: A sign of weakness?

The proponents of zoning have contended that the changing demands of the urban environment can always be met through adjustment of the standard concept. In contrast, those opposed to zoning maintain that increasing complexity and the continual production of variants of one form or another are evidence that zoning has outlived its usefulness. Furthermore, the opponents state that the confusion and the delay generated by the current system, and such inequitable uses as exclusionary zoning, suggest that society suffers more from zoning than it benefits.

Notes

1   J. Delafons, *Land Use Controls in the United States*, p. 19.

2   *New York Times*, April 6, 1913, sec. VIII, p. 1, col. 2 - as quoted in Seymour Toll, *Zoned American*, p. 151.

3   Seymour Toll, *op. cit.*, p. 150.

4   H.M. Lewis, *op. cit.*, p. 262.

5   *Ibid.*, p. 256.

6   Brian Porter, "The Land Use Contract," p. 15.

7   W. Goodman and E. Freund, *Principles and Practices of Urban Planning*, p. 429.

8   The enabling legislation for this device was repealed in August 1977 after repeated claims that it had been used to blackmail developers.

9   L.B. Sagalyn and G. Sternlieb, *Zoning and Housing Costs*, p. 3.

10   *Ibid.*, p.1.

CHAPTER THREE
The Zoning Debate

CHAPTER THREE
The Zoning Debate

In all likelihood, the zoning debate began in North America with the first rumors of its importation in the early years of the twentieth century. The rapid acceptance of land use control laws in the majority of urban areas and their defense by the judiciary proved sufficient to defeat early opponents. This helped its proliferation. The debate, however, has continued.

The pressures of urban development in the second half of this century have uncovered flaws in a number of areas, promoting renewed vigor in the assault on the standard zoning ordinance. Judging by the literature, the tide has definitely changed in favor of the "opponents." Publications of several types and from varied sources offer everything from alternatives and reform to simple lists of "twenty-three reasons why zoning fails." In spite of this continued assault, the zoning ordinance remains. It has been stretched and modified to accommodate some of its critics, but it still occupies the position of the principal land use control in North America.

I.   THE PROS

Zoning protects property values

Its proponents place the central thrust of their arguments on the ability of zoning to protect property values by a "responsible" division of land use. The theory behind the argument holds that as land is immobile, it is, by definition, at the mercy of surrounding uses. But the pricing mechanism of the market can only account for the influence of surrounding uses at the time of purchase. Thus, without adequate controls, uses that generate a negative influence (externality) on proximate land could arise after a purchase and cause a decline in the property's value. The traditional example of this is the glue factory which slips into the heart of the residential neighborhood and decimates property values. This effect is held to be inequitable, and as the mechanisms of the marketplace cannot prevent such an occurrence, government authority is obliged to move in. With a zoning ordinance in place, the mixing of such incompatible issues as residential accommodation and glue factories is prohibited by law. This adds a degree of stability to property values and consequently increases the marketability of all urban property. Hence, "people rely on zoning as a kind of security for their property."[1]   The ordinance, by reducing the number of private land use conflicts arising from the mixing of uses, promotes a more orderly urban environment than was possible under the laws of nuisance. Property values are hence secured, urban chaos is prevented, and the courts are less cluttered.

Zoning betters "the public good"

Another argument in defense of zoning suggests that in its absence not only will different uses be scattered from one corner of the city to the other, on a totally random basis, but also that the market when left on its own will oversupply land for some uses and undersupply it for others - relative to the amounts required for the public good. In essence, this argument would substitute an overall plan for a city's development established in law through the adoption of the zoning ordinance. Communities could thus dictate the location of various enterprises. From this plan, the provision of public services such as sewers, roads, libraries, and schools can be responsibly coordinated with the appropriate land use. Unlike the case of the glue factory abruptly altering the quality of a residential neighborhood, the zoning ordinance

ensures that changing land uses do not result in misalloca-
tions: e.g., schools serving manufacturing areas or industrial
roads catering to residential subdivisions.

Zoning preserves city's character

Zoning's maintenance of the status quo is often credited for
its preservation of a city's character. Adjustment of land use
on strictly economic grounds is viewed as a rather limited
appraisal of society's needs. Most cities can identify areas of
historical importance, the preservation of which would be a
benefit to the public as a whole. Without zoning those areas
would undergo changes in use and style in response to normal
market pressure. Hence, zoning provides interim protection
for areas of historical importance until they are recognized
and afforded special attention.

Zoning controls rapacious developers

A further support for zoning is seen in its ability to place the
developer in a subservient position to the public authority. In
essence, zoning supplies the city planning department with
the power not only to control development, but also to
negotiate within that mandate to ensure that the city in
general will benefit. The primary aspect of this control is
the establishment of different uses in different areas; but
beyond that, the specifications of height, bulk, *fsr*, and lot
dimensions are integral parts of determining what the city
will look like in the future. Furthermore, the provisions for
variances, exemptions, and bonuses are often used to create
parks and plazas that will provide direct benefit to the entire
public rather than just the occupants of the development. In
recent years the zoning ordinance has been viewed as an
extremely important tool of city management in that it
enables civic bodies to shift some of the public costs associated with growth on to private developments.

Zoning ensures majority control of land use

Finally, the proponents of zoning argue that the ordinance
represents an equitable method of land use control. The
majority rules. One or two owners in an area cannot threaten
the property values of their neighbors by indiscriminately
adjusting their land use. Furthermore, when variances or
exemptions are requested, the public forum required by the
zoning ordinance allows the majority to voice their opinion
either for or against a motion.

In short, its proponents argue, zoning is not only a good device for land use control, it is essential for our urban environment. The standard ordinance represents an equitable method of ensuring that the public good is served by accomplishing what, it is said, the market cannot accomplish. Most importantly, it serves the majority and protects property values.

II.   THE CONS

Zoning is based on a faulty premise

On the other side of the coin, the opponents of zoning are armed with an impressive number of faults inherent in the standard ordinance. Their principal argument takes issue with the basis of zoning itself - the process of taking a map of the urban area and establishing one use for area A and another for area B. Zoning is intended to implement a general plan reflecting the community's values for land management. Most critics contend that fortune telling is not sufficiently advanced as a science to allow this.

> The theory behind the current system is that the members of a community can sit down one fine day and determine not only the general nature of its future development but also every detail to such a precise extent that very little need be left to the discretion of an on-going administrative process. The idea that a community can do this rests on the assumption that it has a clear vision of an end state for itself and that little, if anything, can happen to mar that vision. The only way to describe the system, therefore, is to say that it subscribes to a static end state concept of land use control. Plainly that concept is in conflict with reality.[2]

Evidence of zoning's failure in this respect is offered by the numerous examples of variances and exemptions which can be found in any city. Urban growth and its demands are far more dynamic than the adoption of general plans and zoning ordinances would suggest.

Zoning is inflexible

A further criticism is the basic inflexibility of the system. A rigid division of uses cannot account for the variety of tastes and demands that exist in our urban communities. While adjustment of the defined areas is possible within the standard ordinance, the process is complex and awkward, and unlikely to ensure that "unjustified" cases do not slip through. Hence "it could take six months to amend a zoning ordinance to permit emergency or one of a kind uses."[3]   This rigid quality does not apply merely to the division of uses and the appeal procedure. The accompanying regulations covering lot dimensions and bulk, etc., have also continued to grow in detail. This has reached the point where one critic referred to these requirements as a "mathematical girdle" into which an architect has to slip his building.[4]   While this criticism may be somewhat extreme, the minute detail of today's ordinance has been suggested as a cause of deficient site utilization and urban monotony.

Zoning is becoming the tail that wags the planning dog

A criticism of zoning that is receiving increasing support from the planning community itself, is that zoning now totally dominates the planning function as a whole. The increasing complexity of our urban environment has been reflected in the zoning ordinance. Such complexity has fueled the rise in staff personnel needed to enforce the regulations. It has imposed a great increase in the amount of time involved in both the private and public sectors. This has led to the assumption by most people that planning *is* zoning. With as much as 75 per cent of a planning department's time being spent on zoning regulation and enforcement, this definition is rapidly approaching reality.[5]   One critic, to emphasize the time consumption and detail prevalent today, related his experience of "spending three hours discussing the validity of keeping two rather than three llamas on a single piece of property!"[6]

Zoning impedes progress

The opponents of zoning insist that the ordinance improperly preserves the status quo and impedes changes throughout the community - that it generally promotes the continued existence of deteriorating neighborhoods that have a negative effect on the public good. They argue that the economics of the marketplace should be allowed to counteract decaying areas.

Zoning creates legislative inequity

The inequity of the zoning ordinance as a method of land use control is evidenced by its expanding use for exclusionary ends.

> There is no doubt that throughout this nation zoning has been used for exclusionary purposes. In some areas it definitely has been designed to keep out undesirables, socio-economic groups or certain land uses such as multi-family residential or industrial.[7]

Furthermore, opponents contend that the process of public hearings and politician involvement encourages decisions based on personal popularity rather than sound economic principles. This has led to further discrimination through the opposition to an individual because he is "different" rather than disapproval on the grounds of a particular land use.

Zoning lacks an automatic negative feedback mechanism

One of the most persuasive arguments against zoning is the fact that it institutionalizes errors. It is clear that mistakes will be made from time to time as zoning laws are changed to respond to anticipated future developments. However, the cost of error will often fall on "innocent" parties - developers or residents. Accordingly, the planning process is not self-corrective since failures appear as external effects or diseconomies. In effect, planners do not have the incentives to "get it right," nor do they suffer the consequences of "getting it wrong."

Zoning causes corruption and monopolies

The list of arguments against zoning has been steadily growing in recent years. Lists of objections have included anything from the ease with which one can "corrupt" zoning decisions, to zoning's potential to create land monopolies. More recently, the suggestion has been made that zoning has quite simply been outgrown by our urban environment. The times and the pressures of urban land use have changed, and now it is time to end this policy.

> For half a century we have engaged in a kind of legislative Shintoism, worshipping at the shrine of the Standard State Zoning Enabling Act. Zoning

served us well during a period when urban life was simpler and less dynamic. We should honor those who were responsible for its birth and early care...But we do these men and ourselves as well, ultimate honor not by tending their legislative monuments at the end of the by now well-worn legal road they constructed but by carving new trails toward new frontiers to serve an emerging new urban America.[8]

III. THE KEY ISSUES

The traditional arguments in opposition to zoning have avoided direct assaults on the view that zoning protects against the effect of externalities. One of the reasons for this was the lack of empirical research on the subject. It was not until the late 1960s that an empirical study attempted to observe the nature and extent of zoning's effects.

The principal issue to be resolved is the necessity of zoning today. Does zoning protect property values? Is zoning essential or are there alternatives?

The following chapters will present conceptual and empirical analyses in an attempt to resolve these issues.

Notes

1   J. Volrich, Mayor of the City of Vancouver, *The Province*, January 11, 1978, p. 6.

2   J. Krasnowiecki, "The Basic System of Land Use Control," p. 4.

3   D. Woolfe, "Zoning is Doing Planning In," p. 13.

4   J. Baker, "Runaway Zoning," p. 6.

5   Estimated to be 70-80 per cent of total staff members and as much as 75 per cent of a planning department's time.

6   D. Woolfe, *op. cit.*, p. 10.

7   *Ibid.*, p. 11.

8   John Reps, "Requiem for Zoning," p. 67.

CHAPTER FOUR
Empirical Studies

CHAPTER FOUR
Empirical Studies

To complement the conceptual analysis, this chapter reviews the empirical work done on the effect of zoning in the United States.

As many people have pointed out previously, the volume and quality of the empirical research to date is hardly overpowering, due in part to problems related to the availability of data.[1]   However, the work that has been completed offers its most significant contribution to the debate by raising questions regarding the existence and effect of externalities, and the ability of zoning to adjust the market allocation of land uses. In essence, these studies question the mainstays which for years have been taken as axioms by zoning advocates.

I.   CRECINE, DAVIS, AND JACKSON – THE PITTSBURGH CASE

The first study of note was conducted by Crecine, Davis, and Jackson using data obtained from the Department of Planning of the City of Pittsburgh.[2]   The authors introduce their study by pointing out that the urban property   market is "supposedly" characterized by interdependence where externalities retard the efficient operation of the market. It has been observed informally that the associated improvements and detriments affect the price people are willing to pay for an asset. Society's acceptance of this view is manifested in the existence of zoning:

> It so happens that unless social control is exercised, unless zoning is fully and skillfully applied, it is entirely possible for an individual to make for himself a dollar of profit but at the same time cause a loss of many dollars to his neighbors and to the community as a whole, so that the social result is a net loss...Zoning finds its economic justification in that it is a useful device for ensuring an approximately just distribution of costs, forcing each individual to bear his own expenses.[3]

Noting that little empirical research on the effect of zoning had been completed prior to this, the study's intention was to determine the nature and extent of the externality process that zoning was established to control.

Isolating factors causing deterioration of property values

The methodology used is based on the hedonic model of site value first established by Brigham.[4]   Here, the value of a parcel of urban land is hypothesized to depend on a number of factors or variables concerning the site:

- its accessibility to economic activities
- the amenities (including externalities of the site)
- the topography
- the present and future uses
- historical factors affecting utilization

Assuming that these variables determine the value of land, the study postulates that by isolating the effect of all variables, with the exception of the amenities, the effect of externalities on the value of property may be identified. The sale price of the property as recorded by the City of Pittsburgh was considered to be an accurate statement of the value of the property. (Those sales involving relatives or government agencies were eliminated from the sample.) To define the externalities to be included, the study starts with the zoning ordinance itself. Taking the economic function of zoning as expressed by Haig and others to be the removal or mitigation of the influence of negative externalities, it is logical to assume that the ordinance will reflect those items which would cause such diseconomies.[5]   From this, it is reasoned that land values are negatively influenced by all uses below them on the scale established by the zoning ordinance.   "Thus two family dwellings, row houses and apartment houses should exert diseconomies upon single family dwellings.   Row and apartment houses should negatively influence two family dwellings."[6]   The "zoning externality" variable of the equation was expressed as the percentage of the total area occupied by land uses other than single family.

It was further reasoned that additional characteristics could be identified from census data as potential external diseconomies affecting property value.   Thus, measures of delapidation, deterioration, over-crowding, and non-white population were added.   In total, there were twenty-one independent variables used in relation to the market price of single family transactions taken from civic records covering the period 1956 to 1963.

In order to attempt to hold the extraneous variables of accessibility, topography, historic factors, and use constant, the observations were stratified by census tract and zoning category.   In addition, to control for variation in property improvements, the dependent variable was expressed in terms of dollars per square foot.

Surprising results do not support zoning rationale

The research strategy suggested that property values should fall with an increase in the presence of external diseconomies.   Hence, the equation relating the collected data should display this effect, with the coefficients of the independent variables indicating both the extent and direction of the influence of those items postulated to cause externalities.[7]   The results showed that both the magnitude and the direction of the effect (positive or negative) of the independent variables varied across census tract and zoning district.   Although one could expect some variation in magnitude, the variation in the *direction* of the effect runs contrary to the uniformity implied by the rationale behind the zoning ordinance.   In essence, the results suggested that "the use which causes an external *diseconomy* in one district might cause an external *economy* in another."[8]

On a surprising number of occasions, the variables were observed to have a positive effect on property values in spite of the fact that they were predicted to be sources of negative externalities. Of the fifty-five zoning variables observed, thirty-three had positive effects. In the authors' words, this result "cast serious doubt upon the major assumption (the presence of uniform external diseconomies) of one of the basic economic arguments supporting the imposition of restrictive zoning upon the use of urban land."[9]

Pittsburgh data suggest the market is robust - zoning not necessary?

The tentative conclusion reached is that the urban property market is not characterized by great interdependence and externalities. The authors speculate that market mechanisms exist naturally to eliminate such externalities that would arise from the proverbial glue factory on the corner of Portage and Main.

In conclusion, the authors note that limitations in their data and the "crudeness" of their methods make it impossible to claim conclusively that interdependence does not exist. However, they feel that serious doubts are raised about the pervasiveness of externalities as commonly attributed to urban property markets. It follows that equally serious questions are raised regarding the current form of zoning ordinances and ultimately the necessity of this legislation.

The authors and, subsequently, the critics of this study have pointed out a number of weaknesses. Principally, these stem from limitations in the available data. Data were not available for the zoning externalities noted in the ordinance beyond actual land use. Hence, items such as building height, lot size, and yard area were not available for use as potential sources of negative diseconomies. More importantly, data on age, improvements, or structural type of the properties did not exist in a usable form. As these characteristics are generally agreed to have a significant influence on the price of residential property, their absence seriously reduces the explanatory power of the work. Finally, the format of the available data limited the definition of the neighborhood to a city block. Hence, the effect of externalities present in the adjacent block (i.e., on the other side of the street) could not be included in the study as having an effect on the price of the observed single family transactions.

II. RUETER - REFINING ANALYSES
OF THE PITTSBURGH DATA

With these shortcomings in mind, Rueter conducted a refined
and enlarged analysis of the Pittsburgh data.[10]   This study
was expanded to include consideration of the effect of
externalities on two-family dwellings as well as single family
houses.   The sample size was also increased to include
transactions covering the period 1953 to 1969.   To remove
some of the previous shortcomings, the definition of the
neighborhood was expanded to encompass all property within
150 feet of the subject.   This area was taken directly from
the zoning ordinance which stipulated that, in the event of a
zoning change, owners of all properties lying within 150 feet
had to be notified in writing - suggesting that this was the
area likely to be influenced by the change.   In the event that
this was too restrictive, observations were also included up to
a distance of 300 feet.

The number of factors explaining property values was
increased.   In addition to the land use and census data such as
crowding, etc., building and neighborhood characteristics
were added.   Included were such items as height, area and
slope of the property, the building assessment, public land use,
and maximum building height in the neighborhood.   Finally,
the consumer price index was added to account for the effect
of aggregate economic conditions on the observed property
values.

Rueter study confirms Crecine, Davis, and Jackson results

The results reinforced those conclusions reached by Crecine,
Davis, and Jackson (C-D-J).   The effects of externalities
varied in magnitude and direction both across zoning categories and census tract divisions.   In view of the fact that the
same items registered external diseconomies in one area and
external economies in another, doubt is cast upon the proposition that zoning is uniform in its effects.   As in the C-D-J
study, the author felt that the presence of any positive
effects called into question the validity of the principal
economic justification of zoning.

Neither of the Pittsburgh studies claim to be conclusive
proof that externalities do not exist.   However, both claim
that their results indicate the possibility of a natural site
selection mechanism within the market:

> The necessary and sufficient condition for the incidence of externalities is the existence of a similarity of preferences among prospective buyers about desirable and undesirable attributes of the neighborhood. If individual tastes differ among prospective purchasers the interaction of buyers and sellers in their search for the best attainable individual deal serves to minimize the adverse external effects in the market.[11]

The empirical evidence of the Rueter study reinforced the conclusion reached by C-D-J that present zoning procedures are not justifiable. It suggests that current ordinances are far too detailed and that greater reliance should be placed on the pricing mechanism of the market.

III. THE EVIDENCE FROM BOSTON - STULL

The third empirical study specifically investigating the effects of zoning was conducted by William J. Stull.[12] This work took exception to the limitations of the previous studies, particularly in their definition of the neighborhood.[13] Stull's technique consisted of observing the median single family property value for an *entire* community in relation to lower order land use throughout the community, rather than individual transactions. He constructed a sample from forty suburban municipalities in the Boston Standard Metropolitan Statistical Area (SMSA) in 1960. Observations were controlled for physical characteristics such as lot size, age, and the number of rooms per unit. In addition, accessibility to the central business district and "public sector characteristics" such as taxes and school expenditures were included. As in the C-D-J and Rueter studies, the central concern was the environment of the single family homes in the communities, described in terms of lower order land uses. These variables were related to the price of single family dwellings using a multiple regression technique.

Some support for zoning in Stull's work

In contrast to the earlier work of C-D-J and Rueter, the results of this study were consistent with the assumptions of zoning theory, displaying a decline in price associated with the presence of lower order land use. "Homeowners attached the highest value to communities which were predominantly single-family but which also contained a small amount of commercial activity. Homes in communities with large amounts of multi-family, commercial, industrial or vacant land sold at a discount, other things equal."[14]   One interesting characteristic of the data was that up to a point (about five per cent of the total regarded as commercial), such activity was a positive externality, or convenience, to the homeowner.   Beyond the five per cent level, commercial activity led to a decline in property value.

Stull rejects zoning for different reasons

In his concluding remarks, Stull warns against attaching too great a significance to "any single study." In pointing out that his results run directly contrary to those of the two previous works, he nevertheless supports the weakening or ending of current zoning laws. He reaches this conclusion on two grounds. First, there has been a substantial amount of alteration of the zoning ordinance through the granting of a large number of variances. This continual accommodation of market forces must inevitably result in a "configuration of land uses which is not very different from that which would have occurred had zoning never been introduced in the first place."[15]   Secondly, he observes that the incidence of exclusionary zoning aimed at certain socio-economic groups is growing and that the removal or adjustment of this by-law would restrict the power of the municipalities to indulge in such discrimination. In spite of his general opposition to zoning, Stull acknowledges that his empirical findings suggest that the removal of zoning would result in "an undesirable pattern of capital losses on suburban homeowners."[16]

IV.   EVIDENCE FROM ROCHESTER - MASER, RIKER, AND ROSETT

A fourth examination of zoning was published in 1977. This work by Maser, Riker, and Rosett (M-R-R) studies the effects of zoning on the price of land in Rochester, New York.[17] M-R-R looked at two reasons for land use controls: as a protection against externalities generated by offensive uses of land; and as an allocator of land to compensate for the "private sector's short-sighted, narrow perception of the best use."[18] To test for these effects, a sample of real estate transactions was randomly selected from the records of the years 1950, 1960, and 1971. These records were taken from the City of Rochester, which the authors contend is representative of a "medium-sized" American city in terms of population, wealth, social problems, housing, and zoning. The sample consisted of single family, multiple residential, commercial, and industrial property.

Rochester data rejects positive zoning effects

The authors reasoned that the question of whether zoning modifies the allocation of land or not can be studied indirectly by observing the effect of zoning on price. In those instances where land has been over-allocated to a particular use relative to an unregulated market, prices will be depressed in that zoning category. Similarly, where land is under-allocated, there should be an elevation of the price. To test for this and for the effect of externalities, the sample of observations was used, as in the previous studies, to establish an equation relating a variety of factors to the price of land. The model contained "three categories of independent variables: (1) zoning variables, (2) externality variables, and (3) a broad range of factors which jointly predict land prices in the absence of either zoning or externalities."[19] From this format, the zoning variable was tested to see its statistical significance in relation to price and, in eight of the nine tests, no effect on price was attributable to this variable.

M-R-R suggest move toward market solution

These findings suggested to the authors that the restriction of land use in the urban market is not justified by the presence of externalities and that the allocation efficiency suggested by zoning practitioners is *not* effective. The findings suggest that the uniformity of taste implied by the zoning ordinance does not exist. Rather:

> there exists a sufficient diversity of tastes among potential buyers; that is to say, there are buyers who are indifferent to the offensive use (perhaps even value it).[20]

The study concludes with the suggestion that the present system of zoning should be reviewed and adjusted toward land use controls which would place a greater reliance on the courts (e.g., restrictive covenants, fines, etc.).

V.   ZONING IS NOT PROTECTOR OF PROPERTY VALUES

It would appear from these four studies that the traditional justification of zoning as protector of property values is definitely not a clear cut case. In addition, M-R-R question the secondary view that zoning is beneficial through its adjustment of the market's allocation of land uses. While Stull's work gave some credence to the traditional view of zoning with regard to externalities, he supported the others in their recommendation that the zoning ordinance should definitely be reviewed, if not removed.

The smoking gun evidence - Houston

In response to the suggested removal of the zoning ordinances, most critics conjure up hideous descriptions of ravished residential areas and general urban chaos.

> One of the questions which threw some light on the actual effect of zoning in the cities was what would happen if it were suddenly repealed. Planners in a number of cities agree that the areas most likely to be affected rapidly would be the high-class residential districts. They would be penetrated by apartment house developments, and homes would undergo conversion for commercial uses prohibited by current ordinances. Houston, the most notorious example of the unzoned American city, seemed to confirm their predictions.[21]

But aside from its "notorious" reputation, Houston appears to be far from chaotic and has survived the past sixty years without the benefits of a zoning ordinance. Unfortunately, the question of whether Houston has benefitted or suffered because of the absence of zoning has not been subjected to the rigors of empirical examination. The articles that have studied the city remain reflections of the authors' tastes. Hence, some see the city "ugly" and others view it as attractive. (In an appendix to this chapter, Roscoe Jones, Director of City Planning, Houston, Texas, provides a brief discussion of this case.)

Houston isn't totally without control on its land use. Subdivision regulations call for certain lot sizes and set backs, and about two-thirds of the city is covered by some 10,000 restrictive covenants. These deed restrictions, which are, in effect, private zoning, are enforced both individually, and with civic assistance (since 1965). However, attempts to change from this private-civic program to a zoning ordinance

41

were soundly defeated in public referendums held in 1948 and 1962.†

The most comprehensive study of Houston from a land use viewpoint concludes that the non-zoned city does not differ in appearance from what it would have been like if it had been zoned.[22]   This analysis by Bernard Siegan breaks down the city by land uses and compares those in Houston to similar ones in zoned municipalities.   Not only does he observe no substantial problems created by the lack of zoning, the author concludes that the absence of restrictions allows the market to operate more efficiently to the betterment of the city's population.   Siegan suggests that the growing level of criticism directed at zoning is justified and calls for a removal of these ordinances. However, he is not confident that this will happen, stating that the dogma will persist "that if zoning does not work, it is desirable to try more of it."[23]

Even without empirical examination, *the very existence of a large North American city (an area in excess of five hundred square miles and a population of 1.6 million) which can function normally and continue to grow without zoning is a major piece of evidence against the traditional view that zoning supposedly protects against chaos.*

Conclusions from empirical studies

In conclusion, one must agree that the so-called mainstays of zoning justification have definitely not been verified.   The evidence regarding the effect of externalities on property values appears to suggest that the items treated uniformly by the zoning ordinance do not operate in such a fashion in urban land markets.   The observed random operation of these externalities makes it likely that the normal pricing mechanism of the market will minimize any negative effects. This seriously throws into doubt the major economic justification for the imposition of zoning.

---

† Editor's Note: Whether complaints of deed restriction violations are initiated by an individual homeowner or a neighborhood civic association, it is important to realize that the Houston system is a private one. All restrictive covenants reflect voluntary consensual behavior on the part of the concerned buyers and sellers. The buyer is presented with a list of restrictions as part of the sale contract. If he objects, he needn't make the purchase; but if he does, he is bound to abide by the conditions. This is in sharp contrast to the governmental system of zoning, which imposes prohibitions with or without the consent of the affected property owner.

In addition to the effect of externalities, the evidence questions the ability of zoning to adjust the allocation of uses to the "betterment" of society. "Chaos" clearly does not appear to reign if zoning is not in effect.

The evidence regarding the effect of zoning, while not overwhelmingly conclusive, raises questions about a number of factors which were previously taken for granted, and certainly suggest an adjustment in our traditional view of zoning's necessity.

Notes

1   S. Toll, *op. cit.*, p. 300.

2   John P. Crecine et al., "Urban Property Markets: Some Empirical Results and their Implications for Municipal Zoning," pp. 79-99.

3   Robert M. Haig, quoted in J. Crecine et al., *op. cit.*, p. 79.

4   Eugene F. Brigham, *op. cit.*, p. 325.

5   Crecine et al., *op.cit.*, p. 81.

6   *Ibid.*, p. 87.

7   *Ibid.*, p. 87.

8   *Ibid.*, p. 92.

9   *Ibid.*, p. 92.

10   F. Rueter, "Externalities in Urban Property Markets," pp. 313-350.

11   *Ibid.*, p. 336.

12   William Stull, "Community Environment, Zoning, and the Market Value of Single Family Homes," pp. 535-557.

13   It should be noted that these criticisms are aimed primarily at the work performed by C-D-J.

14   W. Stull, *op. cit.*, p. 551.

15   *Ibid.*, p. 553.

16   *Ibid.*, p. 553.

17   S. Maser et al., *op. cit.*, pp. 111–132.

18   *Ibid.*, p. 112.

19   *Ibid.*, p. 122.

20   *Ibid.*, p. 124.

21   S. Toll, *op. cit.*, p. 300.

22   Bernard Siegan, "Non-Zoning in Houston," pp. 71–147.

23   *Ibid.*, p. 143.

Appendix
Houston - City Planning Without Zoning
by Roscoe H. Jones

Many view the City of Houston as very successful. It has grown from a population of 45,000 in 1900 to 384,000 in 1940, 1,232,000 in 1970, and 1,623,000 in 1978, to become the fifth largest city in the United States. During the past six years over 175 national and international corporate headquarter firms have relocated in Houston. Unemployment in August 1978 was 4.2 per cent, compared to San Francisco's 7.3 per cent, New York City's 8.8 per cent, and the Detroit area's 7.1 per cent. Looking at the State of Texas in 1977, the per capita tax burden was $467 compared to $952 for New York and $762 for California. And, according to the Bureau of Labor Statistics' publication entitled *Autumn 1977 Urban Family Budgets*, the cost of an intermediate standard of living for a family of four was $19,972 in New York City, $20,609 in Boston, and only $15,488 in Houston, about 10 percentage points below the national average.

Another indication of success is the subdivision activity in the City of Houston and its extraterritorial jurisdictional area. In 1977, there were 335 subdivision plats recorded which included 52,892 lots or apartment dwelling units covering 18.21 square miles. During the first half of 1978, this increased to 223 subdivision plats with 31,191 lots covering 11.08 square miles of development. And the year 1979 may well set some new records in terms of subdivision activity. There is even a sizable budget surplus each year.

In all fairness, Houston does have some problems, as has any real city. Some view it as sprawling and ugly. There are blighted areas. An endless row of billboards can be found on many of the major thoroughfares, creating a hectic urban scene. But while some observers may view Houston as a sprawling, ugly, mixed-up city, there are numerous examples of outstanding architecture and urban design. The downtown area is very attractive, as is Greenway Plaza, Post Oak-Galleria, as well as many other areas. Most observers would feel, on balance, that Houston is a successful city - a city which, frankly, has its own form of beauty. And yet Houston is unique among U.S. cities in that it has consistently rejected the wisdom of experience and the accepted regulator of orderly growth to become the largest city in the nation without zoning.

I. ZONING REJECTED

The citizens of the City of Houston and its professional planners over the years have of course not been ignorant about zoning. The subject was seriously considered in the 1920s when it was determined that it was not necessary or desirable to impose this exercise of municipal police power upon the citizens. Zoning was again given serious deliberation in 1938 by the Houston City Planning Commission, resulting in studies and recommendations by nationally recognized planning consultants. These studies included a proposed zoning ordinance and map as part of a recommended comprehensive planning program.

In addition, another zoning ordinance and map were prepared and presented to the citizens of Houston in the form of a "straw-vote" election in 1948. This was soundly defeated at the polls. Again in 1962, as part of a comprehensive planning effort, another zoning ordinance and map were prepared and submitted to the citizens in another "staw-vote" election. But again zoning was decisively defeated at the polls. Thus, it is obvious that the subject of zoning has been the target of intensive debate, study, and controversy - and zoning, as a land use control system, has continually been rejected by Houston's citizens through the democratic process.

Growth without zoning?

The question continually raised by knowledgeable people both in the planning profession and otherwise is: How has Houston been so successful in the past and how can its future growth be guided without the use of a zoning ordinance? This is sincerely asked because it is felt that a city without zoning must indeed be a place of chaos with unlimited problems. Indeed, it is no exaggeration to say that this view would garner almost universal acceptance. There are, nevertheless, strong reasons for questioning it.

Market order

The first thing which must be realized is that the market is not merely a set of random, irrational, haphazard occurrences. Although it may appear this way to those not accustomed to seeing the core of rationality amidst the seeming chaos, every action undertaken by business on the market is subject to the test of profit and loss: it is rewarded if in accord with the wishes of consumers and penalized if not.

The "carrot and stick" applies to all business decisions; with regard to the choice of geographical location, this phenomena in Houston has tended to create a reasonably well-ordered pattern. Because of private "marketplace zoning," we find no filling stations at the end of cul-de-sacs; ship channel industries are, naturally, located along the Ship Channel, and so on. There is a certain order in the free market as it determines the land use patterns of the city. The fast growth of Houston has permitted quick adjustment of the land use situation to meet market needs, and has permitted speedy readjustments to the land use pattern.

Without zoning Houston has experienced the development of industrial facilities throughout the community in those areas where the accessibility needs of the particular industry can best be met. Manufacturing has not been constrained and restricted to a few massive industrial areas designated on some master plan and implemented through a zoning ordinance. Many of Houston's suburban areas, which under a zoning ordinance could have been kept free of commercial development, have experienced the development of attractive industries and industrial park-type subdivisions which provide job opportunities closer to home.

Mixed land use patterns

Another of the difficulties with orthodox planning is that it has tended to forbid the juxtaposition of different kinds of land uses. But the Houston experience has shown that the benefits of diversity outweigh those of uniformity.

In older segments of the city, for example, the land use pattern is predominantly single family, with low- to moderate-income housing placed rather closely together. While along major thoroughfares there may be active non-residential commercial developments, many quiet residential neighborhoods can be found which also contain small grocery stores, bars, laundries, and other types of service businesses. These exist only because they are conveniently located to serve a population of general low mobility. Industrial areas may also be found close to older residential areas. While some of these industries may create some pollution within the adjacent residential areas, most do not have a deteriorating effect and, in fact, provide job opportunities for low- to moderate-income groups conveniently located near their homes.

The mixed land use pattern that is found in some sections of the city should, therefore, not be viewed as all bad. In a lower income area, the availability of car-repair services, eating establishments, bars, and such service outlets makes for an "attractive" neighborhood in the sense of convenience for a group that has a low mobility. The ability to establish a business in one's garage or home contributes to easy entry of individuals into the economic system. Many a small business has been started in a home or garage.

Similar results

One paradox is that oftentimes identical land use configurations will result from zoning and non-zoning.

As a tool, zoning is limited in what it can do. As one planning director stated: "In Houston you can have a filling station, a home, an apartment building, and a vacant lot on four corners of an intersection; and in Los Angeles you can have a filling station, a home, an apartment building, and a vacant lot on four corners of an intersection."

Many of the busy thoroughfares in Houston are lined with automobile-oriented retail and service business establishments similar to what many other cities have permitted through long-term administration of zoning ordinances. While most professional city planners deplore strip commercial development, it must be recognized that this provides many important and necessary services in a location most convenient to the general public and particularly to the majority of the population of the city which is highly mobile. Moreover, the areas behind the commercial strip developments have remained quiet and relatively stable residential areas.

II. ANTI-ZONING THEMES

Three-fourths of the built-up area of Greater Houston has come into existence since the end of World War II. This growth has occurred principally in large scale tract developments, and is composed of the typical free-standing home on a lot designed for single family occupancy and ownership. Since land developers and home buyers knew that public control of land use was not available in Houston, those who desired the protection usually provided in a zoning ordinance, turned to private deed restrictions. The developers, in order to maximize their commercial property returns, concentrated their shopping centers and reserved the residential areas for single family use. It is, therefore, not surprising that vast areas of Houston resemble the typical suburban development found in most U.S. cities following the end of World War II.

Zoning is more expensive

In cases where the same results ensue, non-zoning is to be preferred - if only because it is enmeshed in less red tape, and, consequently, cheaper to operate. Apartment development in Houston bears this out.

Since the early 1960s apartment housing has constituted a high percentage of the total dwelling units being constructed. These projects are typically the garden type, from one to three stories with a density range from twenty to thirty dwelling units per acre. Without the restrictions of zoning, sizable vacant tracts have been quickly and appropriately developed into apartment projects to satisfy this expanding market. Houston contains several high-rise, multistory apartment buildings, but these developments continue to be unique; they are designed to serve only a small segment of the very high-income apartment market. In other cities, such vacant tracts might have been rezoned for apartment uses, but only after lengthy and bitter fights. The resultant delay would have frustrated the development of needed dwelling space and increased the cost of this type of housing.

The construction history of townhouses, cluster housing, and planned unit developments also illustrates the greater flexibility possible without zoning. Along with the mushrooming growth of garden-type apartments throughout the city have come other types of housing development designed for single family occupancy and ownership. Offering advantages over the typical single family house and lot combination and apartment style living accommodations, these types of developments are found in all parts of the city. They more efficiently use the land which, even in Houston, is becoming an increasingly expensive commodity. Without zoning, Houston has seen innovations and new approaches to housing development which would have been impossible, or at least many years in coming, under the application of traditional zoning procedures. It is no accident that Houston continues to be recognized for maintaining comparatively low-cost and high-quality housing of all types available in the housing market.

Complexity

Then, there is the sheer complexity of zoning. Although in many places this exercise of the policy power began simply and modestly, it has become enmeshed in reams of bureaucratic red tape.

Simply stated, zoning is the division of a city into separate districts with uniform regulations applying to the land use and buildings within each. Typically, the city is divided into single family, multi family, commercial, and industrial districts. However, some of the more complex zoning ordinances have forty or more different types of districts with very intricate regulations. According to the complaint of one city planner, only the city attorney and he understood the zoning ordinance. This is not surprising. For zoning has become complex, confusing, and often unrelated to any betterment of the city. It has been under attack by many. The original objective, to create a well-ordered city with everything in its place, has not always been achieved. Zoning, per se, does not create the good city.

Racial tensions

Freed from the possible restraints of "large-lot zoning," Houston's low-income and minority groups have been able to move into all types of urban and suburban developments, limited only by their ability to afford the housing they desire. There is no doubt that the accessibility to all types of housing throughout the community by low-income and minority groups has been facilitated by the city's lack of zoning. While the City of Houston is not without its "ghetto" areas, their extent is relatively small. These groups may well have been considerably more over-crowded had "large-lot zoning" and "anti-apartment zoning" been established and administered by the city.

III. PLANNING WITHOUT ZONING

Most people believe that city planning cannot exist without zoning. But the history of city planning in Houston provides a strong counter example.

While zoning legislation has been consistently rejected by Houston citizens, there has been significant and continuous support for planning for the future of the City of Houston. Houston was founded as a bold real estate venture by John and Augustus Allen in 1836. The Allen brothers laid out the city with wide thoroughfares and provided spaces for various public facilities at the head of navigation on Buffalo Bayou. Houston was a planned city in the beginning, and the continuing concern of the people for its future expressed itself in a subsequent master plan prepared by the eminent Boston planner Arthur C. Comey, in 1913. Many of the principal features of Comey's 1913 plan are reflected in the subsequent development of the city, particularly the concept of parkways along Buffalo, White Oak and Brays Bayous. During the 1920s, another master plan of the city was prepared by the firm of Hare & Hare Planning Consultants from Kansas City. This was quite comprehensive and included plans for the development of the city's Civic Center, and for several major thoroughfares.

In 1940, a new City Planning Commission was created along with a City Planning Department to act as the professional staff of the Commission. The city, operating with its first full-time professional planning director and staff, took responsibility for major thoroughfares, freeways, parks, recreational spaces, and other community facilities. This formed the basis of the planning work necessary to guide the growth and development of the city which was to come in the post-World War II years. The program of the Houston City Planning Department has always been strongly oriented toward the control of new land subdivisions within the city as well as the area five miles beyond the city limits.

Besides comprehensive general planning activities, there are a number of functional programs. The traditional planner might view these as fragmented, for they are not all undertaken within the City Planning Department. But such functional planning does contribute to the well-being of the city. Moreover, the Community Development Division of the Office of the Mayor, assisted by the Planning Department, provides numerous studies for the older areas of the city. A number of plans have also been prepared which look to the orderly improvement of the neighborhoods.

Houston planning efforts on the macro scale

For the gross city pattern and metropolitan scale, the City of Houston is planning for its continued growth and redevelopment in the following ways:

a) *Major thoroughfare and freeway plan*
For the 2,000 square mile jurisdictional area, the City Planning Commission has organized a system of major thoroughfares and freeways to give adequate automobile circulation for the present and future. This plan is implemented through subdivision controls and capital improvement expenditures.

b) *General Study Plan for 1990*
While labeled as a "Plan," this document is in reality a graphic illustration of generalized land use and planning forecasts to the year 1990. It is designed to be of interest to those who plan private development and redevelopment projects, to show the potentials for urbanization throughout this area, and to illustrate some specific planning concepts which may or may not be feasible. The study generates public interest in the overall planning processes and in the issues which must be faced in the future.

c) *Capital improvements*
With Houston containing over three-fourths of the metropolitan population, it has had the financial capacity and leadership to undertake major regional projects to ensure the development and distribution of an adequate water supply, drainage system, large-scale wastewater treatment facilities, airports, regional-sized parks and recreational areas, branch libraries, police and fire stations, and other facilities to meet the ever-growing needs of the people. The City Planning Department contributes substantial information toward the formulation of capital improvement programs

designed to meet these regional and metropolitan needs.

d)   *Urban data*
While the activities mentioned above are mostly public in nature, the City Planning Department makes available various statistical data and general information to the private sector which are used as a basis for decision making by the homeowner, the housing and commercial developer, and major industrial concerns.

e)   *Jurisdiction surveillance*
Because of the configuration of the city limits, the extraterritorial jurisdiction of the City of Houston as defined by state law covers the unincorporated territory five miles beyond the city limits - or an area of almost 2,000 square miles. The City Planning Department maintains a constant overview of development activity and factors which affect demographic and socio-economic conditions within the area. All applications for the creation of new political subdivisions or additions thereto are reviewed. Recommendations are regularly formulated to implement the city's continuing annexation policy.

Houston planning efforts on the micro scale

The above has briefly explained the activities of the Houston City Planning program as it relates to planning on a large metropolitan scale. On the parcel-by-parcel, block-by-block, or micro-scale, the following steps are being taken:

a)   *Subdivision control*
The policies of the City Planning Commission have secured an adequate street system and subdivision layout within the city's 509 square miles and in the jurisdictional area of some 2,000 square miles. These subdivision control policies, carried out since 1940, assure not only a good basic layout, but provide for set back of buildings and minimum lot size. Three-fourths of the built-up areas of Houston have been built under subdivision control, the importance of which cannot be underestimated. While the city does not have zoning, it has many police power regulations which contribute to its proper growth and development. Zoning is the exercise of a city's police power regulations by dis-

tricts. But police power regulations can also be applied on a city-wide basis for a given use or situation.

b)   *Private street ordinance*
     All apartment developments with buildings extending more than 300 feet from a public street are reviewed by the City Planning Commission. In effect, the subdivision controls are extended to major apartment developments and an internal private street system is assured for good development. There is also a fence ordinance in which junk yards are required to be blocked off to help reduce their unsightly appearance.

c)   *Off-street parking ordinance*
     This requires that residential developments provide off-street parking spaces meeting adopted design standards with the number of spaces varying according to the number of bedrooms. Several years ago, before the apartment boom got underway, the City of Houston established off-street parking requirements for apartments on a one space per apartment basis. More recently, this was increased to two parking spaces for a three-bedroom unit and to one and one-third spaces for an efficiency apartment. These requirements far exceed those of many cities.

d)   *Capital improvement program*
     In a fast-growing area with limited capital funds, the control of capital improvements is an important city planning tool. Park and recreation improvements, street and sewer improvements, etc., can be coordinated with the timing of private developments and can be used as an effective tool in up-grading the older areas. The provision of vest pocket parks and streets, drainage, and sewer improvements in the older areas also makes major contributions to better living for low-income people.

e)   *New approaches*
     The City Planning Commission, while pleased and proud of the Houston city planning program, is continually hard at work trying to make improvements. It is hoped that as the city planning program of Houston further develops, assisted by federal aids such as community development demonstration and research grants, that new approaches to land use controls and measures of "goodness" of a given pattern can be found. Houston's

city planning program is attempting to better relate the physical goals of planning, such as order and beauty, with the social and economic goals of greater freedom of choice for all, closer home to work relationships, etc. The plan is always developing; it is never static.

City planning as forecasting

Theoretically, city planning seeks to determine municipal goals and objectives. Based on a study of its past, present, and future trends, it proposes meaningful and feasible courses of action. But too often city planners approach their task from a utopian viewpoint that results in a plan more contoured to daydreams than honest recognition of the democratic context of the U.S. city. It is important that the city planner and official fully appreciate that they do not have complete autocratic control of the shape and destination of the urban environment. It is important for them to remember that the well-ordered city consists of more than a uniform, sterile, segregated land use pattern. The city's job opportunities, the availability of public facilities and service, the freedom of choice for all, are also hallmarks of the "good city." Too often planners have attempted to create a land use pattern which from their middle class value system might be termed "well ordered" and "good," but which has frustrated the achievement of other social and economic goals of equal, if not greater, importance.

Rather than proposing a rigid plan enforced by a rigid land use control system, the planner can gain more by forecasting the future of his urban area and preparing plans for public facilities and services to meet changes. He can also provide suggestions and even persuasion for the private sector to conform to the forecast if desirable, or to alter the forecast.

In Houston, the effort has been to forecast the growth patterns in order that the city government may supply the necessary municipal facilities and services at the right time, at the right size, and at the right place. This form of a land use management is based on a philosophy of cooperating with private developers, as they contribute to the growth and development of the city. Local government has accepted the responsibility to meet the municipal service and facility needs of its people. Timely information has also been supplied about the future of city growth patterns so that individuals, and other governmental agencies could make better decisions.

The success of Houston is based in part on cooperative municipal government working with all interests in the city, imposing minimal regulations and making only prudent expenditures.

Private deed restrictions

Another aspect of government activity is the cooperative effort of the city in helping private landowners enforce their deed restrictions. Historically, Houston, a city without zoning, has tended to rely on private deed restrictions, particularly in the new residential developments following World War II. In 1965, following the defeat of zoning in 1962, the people of Houston secured a *State Enabling Act* to permit the city to participate in the enforcement of deed restrictions. The city's participation has been helpful. Often times, merely calling on a person attempting to use his property in violation of the deed restrictions has been sufficient to stop such behavior.

While the City of Houston and its people have failed to embrace zoning over the years, they certainly have embraced the system of deed restrictions warmly. For those who believe tight land use control is desirable, the private deed restriction has provided the answer. Restrictive covenants have been a viable tool in private land use control, but this is not to say that this tool has been a perfect one. While many deed restrictions have provided for automatic renewal and while many have been reinstated by securing 100 per cent approval of the affected property owners, there are others which have expired or not been renewed. Some have failed because they have not been kept in full force. Presently, it is not known exactly how much of the city is covered by deed restrictions. However, it is estimated that about two-thirds of the city is covered by some 10,000 such covenants. It has been noted that the physical appearance and land use pattern of the City of Houston is similar to other large U.S. cities and deed restrictions have, of course, assisted materially in creating the general land use uniformity so noticeable in the suburban areas. Since 1965, the City of Houston, pursuant to laws enacted by the Texas Legislature, has been given an opportunity to assist individual property owners in their efforts to protect the validity of their particular deed restrictions and prevent their violation in the area of land use. Only by a most exhaustive research effort, however, could one state that Houston's approach to land use control through participation in the enforcement of private deed restrictions does not reasonably compare with the zoning approach of other cities. In fact, the deed restriction approach in practice may well be superior to zoning as actually practiced by most cities. Too often zoning is referred to in its idealized form and the practical realities are ignored. But zoning in practice is *also* far from a perfect tool. Certainly the private deed restriction approach of Houston is worthy of careful study and long-term evaluation as a democratic land use guidance system more attuned to the dynamics of the ever-changing urban community.

Although the City Planning Department does not have direct control over the establishment and enforcement of private deed restrictions, they are certainly consulted by the developers, and the Department works closely with some 150 civic clubs and associations throughout the Houston area. Indeed, the absence of zoning with its consequent reliance on deed restrictions has brought many neighborhoods together in formal civic associations to work for the continuance of their deed restrictions and for the improvement of the neighborhood.

IV. SUMMARY AND CONCLUSIONS

While this paper is not a final nor definitive statement, it is hoped that it has brought a clear understanding of the Houston city planning program and what it has accomplished and hopes to accomplish without zoning. The following summarizes and suggests conclusions:

A. Twice the voters of Houston have decisively turned down zoning legislation. Planners and city officials have, therefore, implemented programs which did not include zoning.

B. Houston's land use pattern on the whole is not greatly different than that from other U.S. cities. Certainly there are land use problems, but similar difficulties can be found elsewhere.

C. Houston has grown and developed largely after World War II. This has meant that it has developed with higher standards and levels of affluency than existed in older cities. Consequently, many of the land use abuses which zoning was designed to correct are not prevalent nor pronounced in Houston.

D.   The mixed land use pattern in low-income areas where deed restrictions have expired or were never instituted is not an evil or bad condition. On the contrary, it may well provide convenience to work places, shopping facilities, and social activity centers for people who are relatively immobile.

E.   The rapid growth of Houston has challenged private enterprise to adapt to change and meet new market demands. The city, by anticipating changes, has been able to adapt streets, utilities, and other public facilities and service systems to meet the changes. Indeed, we might suggest that city-wide dynamism, low employment rates, and other favorable factors prevail in Houston because the private investor has been unhampered by cumbersome zoning requirements.

F.   The lack of zoning in Houston may loom gloomingly large in the minds of many professional planners as a major deficiency, even a disaster. However, before Houston and its non-zoned city planning is condemned, it is well to appraise the city as it really exists: with ample job opportunities for all; featuring a fresh and dynamic, forward-looking character, akin to a frontier boom town, but enjoying the freedom to create new approaches; a good city to be enjoyed by all. Has the absence of zoning hurt Houston or any of its people? It would be difficult to conclude that planning without zoning has not worked reasonably well to date. And with local determination to find new answers to every pressing problem, the future of Houston without traditional zoning looks bright indeed.

CHAPTER FIVE
The Evidence on Zoning:
A Canadian Example

CHAPTER FIVE
The Evidence on Zoning:
A Canadian Example

In this chapter, additional empirical evidence is presented to aid in the assessment of zoning. The studies discussed here are Canadian in origin, taking their data from observations in the City of Vancouver. In contrast to the U.S. studies, these seek to isolate the effect of zoning by examining certain examples of rezoning in an urban area.

I. INTRODUCTION: BACKGROUND, RATIONALE, AND PURPOSE

Rezoning land in urban areas is becoming increasingly contentious. On the one hand, citizens dislike the windfall profits that landowners reap from rezoning, and, on the other hand, neighbors of rezoned properties talk of declining property values and decay. It is sometimes seen as an open invitation to speculators and the beginning of the end for a stable single family neighborhood. Rezoning is simultaneously viewed as an act creating value on subject properties and taking it away from adjacent holdings. Remedies proposed include moratoria on rezoning and taxing away the resulting increment in land values (the so-called unearned increment).

Because emotion runs high in such localized questions, it is often difficult to separate the real effects of rezoning from those imagined, perceived, feared, or desired. This chapter addresses a number of facets of rezoning and its impact on land values using empirical evidence drawn from registered real property transactions in the City of Vancouver.

Two quite different studies will be reviewed here. The first deals with a survey of 529 properties that were traded during the 1966-1972 period, 267 of which were in areas where zoning was unchanged and, therefore, provide a control group. Nine different types of rezoning were considered and their impacts on land values observed.

The second study focuses on a specific area of Vancouver known as Kerrisdale, a stable middle and upper middle income single family neighborhood. In the heart of Kerrisdale lies a thriving commercial area around which can be found a layer of medium density apartments. In 1961 this zone was extended into the surrounding single family dwelling area. A total of 748 transactions were recorded in the rezoned and surrounding single family areas, as well as in four control districts in Kerrisdale. These sales provide insight into the pattern of changes in property values both spatially (e.g., proximity to the affected vicinity) and over time. The transactions span the years from 1955 to 1966 and so provide a long enough time period to see the impact of the rezoning and of the expectations prior to the rezoning.

II. REZONING IN VANCOUVER, 1966-1972: AN OVERVIEW

Purpose of the study

There was growing concern about windfall gains realized by property owners as the result of rezoning land to a higher use. This led the Finance Committee of the Vancouver City Council to ask the Director of Finance to explore the likely effects of an "added value" tax on windfall gain resulting from such a policy. Accordingly, in the summer of 1974, Mr. Kenneth Tunnicliffe undertook this study. The general proposition addressed by Tunnicliffe, and the proposition of central concern to the City of Vancouver, was the following:

> Since the power to rezone is at the discretion of the Vancouver City Council, any increase in property value that results from a decision to rezone should accrue to the City.[1]

This proposition implies two things, which were the focus of Tunnicliffe's work:

1. that rezonings do in fact have an influence on property values; and

2. that the city is justified in its claim to any increased values that have resulted from rezoning decisions.

Clearly, for the City of Vancouver to be able to tax the so-called "unearned increment" (or added value in the Finance Committee's terms), such an increment must be shown to exist. This was Tunnicliffe's first objective and the one of interest to the present study. His secondary objective of delimiting the bounds within which the City of Vancouver could levy such a tax is beyond the scope of the inquiry here.

Structure and methodology

In theory, and under appropriate assumptions concerning supply and demand, rezoning can lead to significant increases in the value of real property, and more specifically in land values. The question then becomes an empirical one. To study the impact of rezoning on real property values, the 1966-1972 period was chosen because of the existence of a consistent data base (beginning in 1966) available from the City of Vancouver assessment rolls, which record all trans-actions as well as the assessed values of land and improve-ments. Since the study was conducted during the calendar year 1974 - and there exists a two-year lag in assessments - 1972 provided the most recent terminal year.

There are over 100,000 properties in the City of Van-couver. Of these fewer than 0.5 per cent were in areas that were rezoned between 1966 and 1972. All affected proper-ties were originally intended to be included in the study. However, lack of data precluded using the entire collection. A total of 446 properties were available representing 21 different rezoning types. Table 1 summarizes the sample depicting both the pre-rezoning and post-rezoning zones.

Some caveats about the sampling procedure are in order. The transactions in Table 1 are those affected by rezoning. To explore the impact, the study had to develop a sample of non-rezoned properties to serve as a control group. This was done using information from the City of Vancouver Assessment Office in areas that were similar to the rezoned areas *before* rezoning, but were not subsequently changed. Assessment records spanning the period 1965-1974 were sampled. This began with 1965 because it was the earliest year that would provide a consistent method of assessment through 1974, when the study was being conducted. Two periods, therefore, were of interest: 1966-1972 for rezoning; and 1965-1974 for assessment records. This reflects the fact that the 1972 rezonings would not appear on assessments until 1974 since there was a two-year lag between assessments and market observations (e.g., 1967 transactions would be reflected in 1969 assessments, and so on). Thus, to look at the impact of rezoning activity in the City of Vancouver during the period 1966-1972, assessment records from the period 1965 through 1974 were used to give before and after views of property values and to present a long enough time period to assemble statistically significant numbers of affected and control group properties.

Table 1
MATRIX OF INITIAL PRE- AND POST-REZONING TYPES

		Post-Rezoning							
		RS-1	RS-2	RM-3	C-2	CRM-2	M-1	M-2	CD-1
Pre-	RS-1		87	1	15				42
Rezoning	RS-2	4			1				
	RT-2			40	18				3
	RM-3				13		9		7
	C-1	2		1	9		4		1
	M-1	49			31	107		2	

RS-1	Residential, low density	C-2	Strip street commercial
RS-2	Residential, medium density, single family	CRM-2	Mixed commercial and multi-family residential
RT-2	Duplex residential and semi-detached		
RM-3	Residential, medium density, multi-family	M-1	Industrial, light
C-1	Neighborhood commercial	M-2	Industrial, heavy
		CD-1	Comprehensive

Source: K.W. Tunnicliffe, p. 53.

The resulting total of 446 transactions presented in Table 1 did not have sufficient numbers of properties in some of the cells to allow any statistically meaningful analysis. The sample was, therefore, revised to eliminate types of rezonings with very few observations such as C-1 to CD-1. Other observations were also deleted where properties were replotted. The resulting sample appears in Table 2 and consists of 267 observations. An additional 262 control group observations were selected resulting in a total sample of 529 properties.

Table 2
REVISED MATRIX OF PRE- AND POST-REZONING TYPES*

		Post-Rezoning					
		RS-1*	RS-2	RM-3	C-2	CRM-2	CD-1
Pre-Rezoning	RS-1		86		6		10
	RT-2			11	8		
	RM-3				10		
	M-1	26			17	93	

* See Table 1 for definitions.
Source: K.W. Tunnicliffe, p. 61.

Organizing these observations by type of rezoning led to the creation of Table 3 which sets out the distribution of the 529 properties.

Table 3
REZONINGS BY TYPE*

Type	Rezoning	No. Rezoned	Control	Total
1	RS-1 to RS-2*	86	86	172
2	RS-1 to C-2	6	6	12
3	RS-1 to CD-1	10	10	20
4	RT-2 to RM-3	11	13	24
5	RT-2 to C-2	8	10	18
6	RM-3 to C-2	10	5	15
7	M-1 to RS-1	26	27	53.
8	M-1 to C-2	17	15	32
9	M-1 to CRM-2	93	90	183

* See Table 1 for definitions.
Source: K.W. Tunnicliffe, p. 64.

One last caveat needs to be discussed. The assessed values of the 529 observations are supplied by the City of Vancouver Assessment Office. Accordingly, it is necessary to test the reliability of these assessed values against market observations. Of the total of 529 properties, 118 had been traded at arms-length during the 1965-1972 period (e.g., roughly 22 per cent). These recorded transactions provide the basis for testing. To do this, simple statistical techniques were used. It was found that the correlation between market values and assessed values was very close to 1.0, implying almost a perfect fit. Thus, the use of assessment records appeared to be well founded.

Findings

Having established the reliability of the assessment information, it was possible to perform a number of tests to determine: (1) if rezoning did in fact have a significant effect on property values; (2) what were the likely magnitudes of these effects?

Using simple regression analysis, it was relatively easy to demonstrate that the rezoned properties changed in value over the 1965-1974 period at substantially different rates from the properties of similar type in the control groups. However, this test merely looked at the overall effect of rezoning. This masks the effects of different types of the phenomena. Accordingly, the properties were broken into the nine classes of rezoning which appear in Table 3, and the changes in values were compared within each. This allowed a finer focus on the effect of rezoning by type. Tables 4 and 5 set out the relative importance of zoning on changes in property values. Table 4 separates the effect of rezoning from other factors affecting properties during the 1965-1974 period.

Table 4

RELATIVE IMPORTANCE OF REZONING BY TYPE, 1965-1974

Type	(1) Est. Coefficient Control	(2) Est. Coefficient Zoning	(3) % (3)=(2)/(1)
1	2.7130	0.1017	3.75
2	2.8296	1.8093	63.94
3	2.8667	2.8266	98.60
4	2.4250	3.9299	162.06
5	3.1723	1.7758	55.98
6	5.1722	-2.2511	-43.52[†]
7	2.9045	3.3469	115.23
8	2.5271	0.2228	8.82
9	2.6248	1.7993	68.55

Source: K.W. Tunnicliffe, p. 66.

[†] Editor's Note: This is a correction of a typographical error in the source.

Column 3 calculates the relative effect. Entries in Column 3 close to 100.00 imply that zoning and other factors weighed equally in affecting property values. Values close to 0.00 imply that zoning was overshadowed by other factors affecting property markets in general. Values over 100.00 connote greater importance of rezoning compared with other factors. Thus, Type 1 rezoning (from RS-1 to RS-2) resulted in relatively insignificant changes in property values, especially when compared with general market factors. This is reflected in a Column 3 entry of 3.75 which is close to 0.00. On the other hand, Type 4 rezoning (from RT-2 to RM-3) produced a figure of 162.06, implying that zoning factors were almost twice as important as general factors.

Another way to summarize these findings is to calculate the average annual percentage increase in rezoned and control group properties over the period 1965–1974. Table 5 presents these figures. Once again Column 3 provides a convenient measure of the relative change in growth rates attributable to rezoning. A number of interesting observations can be made from these data. First, not all rezonings to supposedly higher uses led to increases in values. Type 1 rezoning led to almost no appreciable increase in value; the same is true for Type 8 (from M-1 to C-2). Most strikingly, Type 6 rezoning (from RM-3 to C-2) actually led to a very significant decline in property values of roughly 7.4 per cent per year compounded over the period.

Table 5

AVERAGE YEARLY PERCENTAGE CHANGE IN VALUE, 1965–1974

Type	(1) Control (%)	(2) Rezoned (%)	(3) Change (%) (3)=(2)-(1)
1	11.7	12.1	0.4
2	12.3	18.6	6.3
3	12.4	21.3	8.9
4	10.4	22.8	12.4
5	13.7	19.4	5.7
6	20.0	12.6	-7.4
7	12.6	22.6	10.0
8	10.9	11.9	1.0
9	11.3	18.0	6.7

Source: K.W. Tunnicliffe, p. 67.

The implications reached from these findings are important and not necessarily those that might have been anticipated beforehand. First, looking at the overall picture in Table 5, it was observed that rezoning did have an impact on property values during the 1965-1974 period. Second, and of even greater importance, when looking behind these aggregate figures it was observed that the impact of rezoning varied dramatically, depending upon the type under consideration. Some changes such as from duplex (RT-2) to medium density apartments (RM–3) led to large increases in assessed property values (Type 4). In contrast, rezoning properties from medium density apartments (RM-3) to medium density commercial (C-2) led to significant declines in property values (Type 6). In addition, rezoning from heavy industrial (M-1) to single detached (RS-1) (Type 7) led to increases in property values matched only by rezoning from duplex to medium density apartments (Type 4).

Therefore, it appears quite justifiable to warn against generalizing about the impact of rezoning. Allowing some supposedly higher uses (such as from RM-3 to C-2) led to declines in property values, not increases, as one would have expected (Type 6). Other such changes had little if any impact (Types 1 and 8). Thus, the only general statement that can be made from these findings is *avoid generalizing*. It is essential to examine each type of rezoning in its own right before making any statements of *fact* about the direction and magnitude of change.

Qualifications

As with any empirical study, the results can be only as good as the data. But in this case, one can be relatively confident that the assessments were reliable and useful for the purposes. To test this more rigorously would have required sampling transactions from the records of the Land Registry Office (L.R.O.), an expensive and time-consuming task. Given the high degree of correlation between the observed transactions and the assessed values, this does not appear to be justified, though to be absolutely sure (or as absolutely sure as one can be with actual data) resorting to L.R.O. data would have been preferable. Second, one might have extended the sample beyond the City of Vancouver to other municipalities. Once again this would have been an expensive and costly proposition and given the sponsorship by the City of Vancouver, unwarranted. However, the study can be replicated quite easily in other municipalities and such replication is most desirable to test the generality of the methods and conclusions set out above.

III.   REZONING IN VANCOUVER:
   THE CASE OF KERRISDALE, 1961

One of the strongest conclusions that can be drawn from the works described above is that the specifics of each rezoning must be studied in some depth if any understanding of the dynamics of the changes in property values is to be gained. With this in mind, in 1975 a study was undertaken of the Kerrisdale area of Vancouver,† where a major rezoning from single family detached (RS-1) to medium density apartments (RM-3) occurred in 1961. Where the city-wide study concentrated on identifying whether or not rezoning affected property values, the Kerrisdale study sought to explore the dynamics of land value change both over time and over space. Of interest were the timing of speculative transactions and the spatial spread of property value effects (both positive and negative). The details of the Kerrisdale rezoning are presented below, and the results and methods discussed in some depth.   The strengths and weaknesses of this study are also discussed, and in a concluding section the results are examined to determine their implications for zoning and land use controls in the future.

Background, history, and purpose

The Kerrisdale study was more narrowly focused than the city-wide analysis of rezoning done by Tunnicliffe.   It examined the impact of zoning on speculation and, therefore, on neighborhood stability as well as the impact of rezoning on adjacent properties that have not been rezoned (e.g., the externalities argument). To examine these dimensions it was necessary to find a sample which was fairly large in scale and which constituted a change from a lower to a higher use. Such uses are supposedly incompatible and, therefore, zoning protection is presumably needed to minimize or eliminate negative externalities.

Two cases existed for study as a result of an August, 1958 report to City Council by the Vancouver Technical Planning Board. That report recommended that the city give

---

† Editor's Note: This examination was made by Goldberg and Horwood, the authors of the present volume. What follows is the initial report of the results uncovered in that study.

serious consideration to decentralizing residences away from the high density West End immediately adjacent to the Vancouver Central Business District (CBD). Two specific regions suggested by the report which were subsequently rezoned were the area at East 43rd Avenue and Fraser Street (an old retail area) and the Kerrisdale area at West 41st Avenue at Yew Street (see Map 1 of Vancouver), surrounding the existing medium density residential zone ((RM-3 zone) see Map 2 of Kerrisdale). Both areas received additional study by the planning authorities in the city and were eventually rezoned. The Fraser Street and East 43rd Avenue change, however, never gained market acceptance as it was not a prime residential location. As a result, even though it was rezoned to RM-3 from RS-1, it did not develop as an apartment zone and thus had to be eliminated from the study.

Map 1
GREATER VANCOUVER AREA

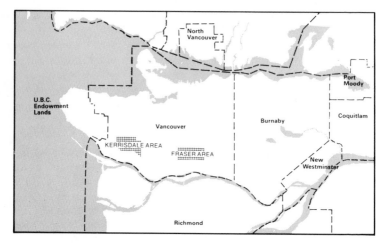

But the Kerrisdale alteration did gain instant market acceptance. Accordingly, it provides the focus for this study. As there is interest in both changes in real property values over time (as a result of the anticipation of rezoning and of rezoning itself) as well as over space (as a result of the supposed negative externalities that exist between apartment and single family houses), the concern here is with the timing of the rezoning as well as its location and geographic impact.

Map 2

RM-3 ZONING IN KERRISDALE

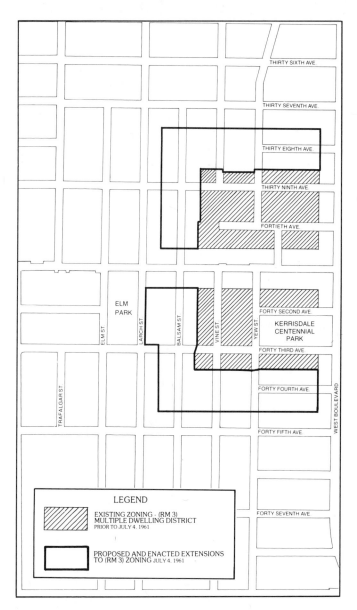

THIRTY SIXTH AVE.

THIRTY SEVENTH AVE.

THIRTY EIGHTH AVE.

THIRTY NINTH AVE.

FORTIETH AVE.

FORTY SECOND AVE.

ELM PARK

KERRISDALE CENTENNIAL PARK

ELM ST

LARCH ST

BALSAM ST

VINE ST

YEW ST

FORTY THIRD AVE.

TRAFALGAR ST

FORTY FOURTH AVE.

WEST BOULEVARD

FORTY FIFTH AVE.

FORTY SEVENTH AVE.

LEGEND

EXISTING ZONING - (RM 3)
MULTIPLE DWELLING DISTRICT
PRIOR TO JULY 4, 1961

PROPOSED AND ENACTED EXTENSIONS
TO (RM 3) ZONING JULY 4, 1961

Map 3 – KERRISDALE STUDY AREA

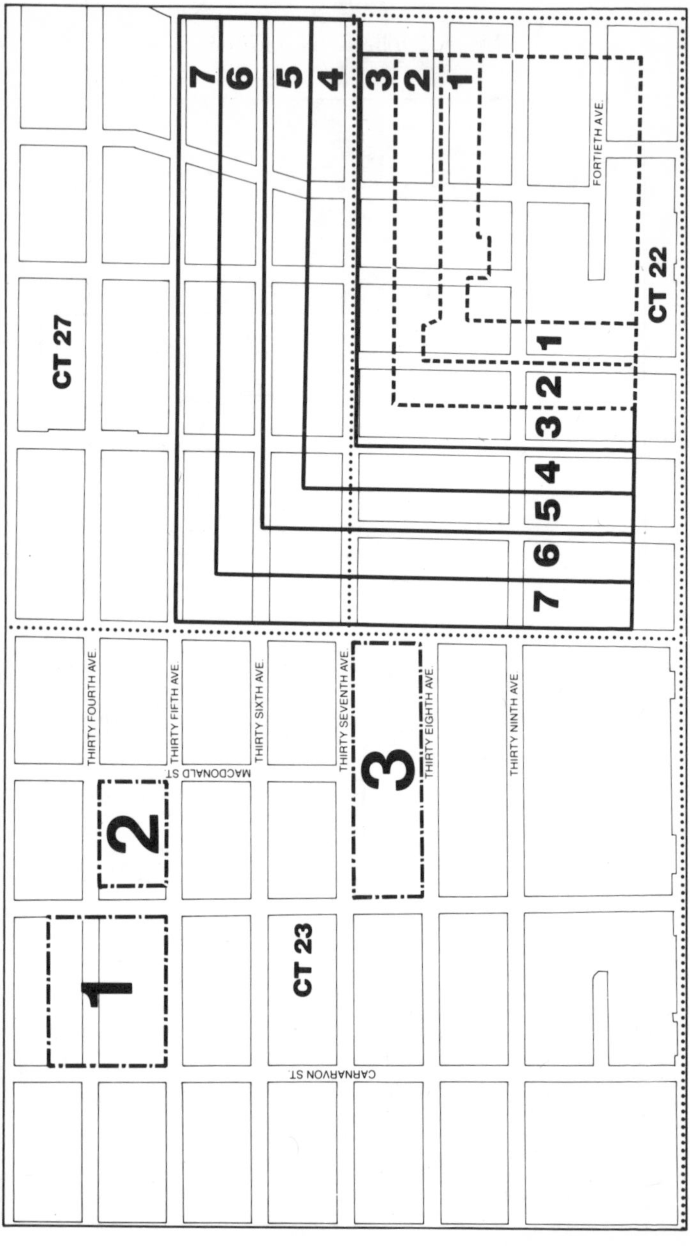

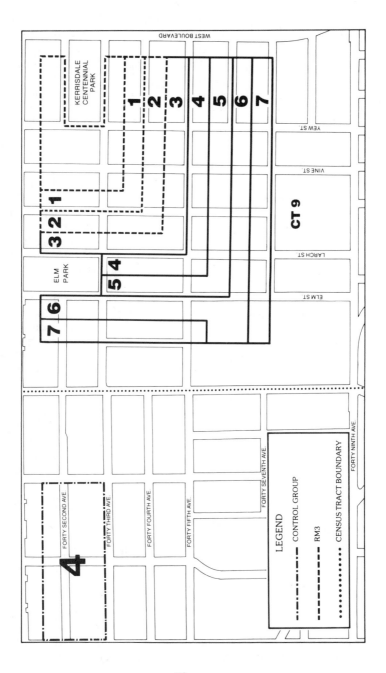

Following upon the August, 1958 report of the Technical Planning Board, further studies were conducted on Kerrisdale. City records show that the final public hearing required under the Vancouver Charter of Zoning By-laws was conducted on May 15, 1961, and By-law #3927 was given final approval by Council on July 4, 1961, at which time the area shown on Map 2 was rezoned from RS-1 (single detached housing) to RM-3 (multi-family medium density housing).

Procedures

In light of these events it was decided to break the study into three time periods: *Period 1* - from January 1, 1955 to November 30, 1958, when the Technical Planning Board report was considered; *Period 2* - from December 1, 1958 to June 30, 1961, when the rezoning by-law was enacted; and *Period 3* - from July 1, 1961 to December 31, 1966. The endpoints of January 1, 1955 and December 31, 1966 were chosen because it was possible to get consistent information from the Vancouver City Assessor's record during this period. However, to keep the periods roughly equal in length, transactions beyond March 31, 1963 were ignored. Differences in format both before 1955 and after 1966 made consistent data gathering extremely difficult, and unless consistency could be maintained, little validity could be attached to any subsequent findings.

It was also necessary to delimit a meaningful study area to look at the effects of rezoning on adjacent properties. To do this, a series of concentric rings surrounding the existing RM-3 zone in Kerrisdale were developed. Each ring was one-half block in width. A total of seven such rings were identified, the first two of which were rezoned, the remaining five of which remained RS-1. Finally, a control group of properties was needed which was similar to the rezoned area and its adjacent rings, but which was sufficiently far away to preclude any spillover effects of the rezoning. Four such control groups were identified in the Kerrisdale area within a fifteen block radius of the rezoning. These areas are all set out on Map 3 which summarizes the foregoing discussion on the study area.

Given the appropriate time period and geographic study area, the final element in developing the methodology was the determination of a suitable data source for market transactions. Several sources were available: the L.R.O. which records actual transaction prices for all transfers of property duly registered with it; *Teela*, a real estate market service that gathers transaction information from the L.R.O. on a semi-monthly basis; and the City Assessor's records which also show actual arms-length transactions for every property on the assessment rolls.

As was mentioned before, using L.R.O. records is extremely time consuming and difficult. Moreover, the information is limited to the recorded transaction price, the purchaser and vendor, and the legal address. The Assessor's records, in contrast, yield information on transaction price, lot size, assessed value of land and improvements, legal address, and assessment roll number. They were readily available in a consistent form over the study period as noted previously. Accordingly, the decision was made to use assessment records.

Other items of information gathered were the registration of Rights to Purchase, Assignment of Rights to Purchase, Sub-rights to Purchase, Assignment of Sub-rights to Purchase, and sales to non-resident owners who were not builders. These variables were used as proxies for speculative activity. (Such transactions are characteristic of investors/speculators, not residential owners.)

Table 6 sets out in summary form the numbers of transactions and properties that appeared in the study. Property transactions were recorded for all seven rings and for the four control areas (e.g., a 100 per cent sample) with one exception: no transactions were obtained for the rezoned areas after the rezoning since the study was not concerned with multiple family housing but only with the effects on existing single family housing. There was a total of 979 properties in the study areas and 744 observed transactions over the study period. In addition, 185 rights were registered and 43 sales to non-resident owners were recorded.

Results

Tables 6 through 9 set out in summary form the principal findings of the study. The transactions were analyzed by location (e.g., ring location or control area as shown on Map 3), by period (e.g., before rezoning study, during study, and after rezoning), and by size of lot (greater or less than 5,000 square feet). Properties were analyzed by lot size because preliminary analyses showed that grouping tended to blur the price changes, since larger lots sell for higher prices. Thus, if one ignored lot sizes and if the proportion of larger lots decreased in the sample, over time one might spuriously show declining prices when, in fact, only the proportion of large lots were decreasing.

Table 6

SUMMARY OF PRICE CHANGES
(per cent)

	Period 1 through Period 2* (Jan. 1, 1955 – June 30, 1961)	Period 2 through Period 3 (Dec. 1, 1958 – March 31, 1963)	Period 1 through Period 3 (Jan. 1, 1955 – March 31, 1963)
LOT SIZE LESS THAN 5000 SQ.FT.			
Non-Control Group			
Rezoned lots	6.8	20.8	29.0
Non-rezoned lots	23.2	-0.7	22.3
Ring 1	19.9	13.7	36.2
2	1.6	23.5	25.5
3	33.4	-6.3	24.9
4	23.6	-32.4	-16.5
5	25.7	5.8	33.0
6	18.7	35.7	61.1
7	26.6	11.3	40.9
Control Group			
All lots	23.5	-17.6	1.8
Ring 1	20.9	-21.5	-5.2
2	-	-	-
3	-	-	-
4	28.9	-0.7	28.0
LOT SIZE GREATER THAN OR EQUAL TO 5000 SQ.FT.			
Non-Control Group			
Rezoned lots	-4.6	65.3	57.7
Non-rezoned lots	15.8	-10.2	4.0
Ring 1	-10.6	49.5	33.7
2	-0.5	82.9	81.9
3	13.1	-23.3	-13.3
4	14.6	-7.2	6.4
5	23.0	-20.1	-1.7
6	13.3	3.2	17.0
7	18.4	-12.1	4.1
Control Group			
All lots	4.8	0.6	5.4
Ring 1	9.9	-100.0	-100.0
2	10.7	7.8	19.3
3	18.7	-12.7	3.6
4	-5.8	7.8	1.5

Notes: * Period 1 – January 1, 1955 to November 30, 1958
Period 2 – December 1, 1958 to June 30, 1961
Period 3 – July 1, 1961 to March 31, 1963

For each period, the mean (average) price was calculated for all rezoned and all non-rezoned properties (Tables 7, 8, 9). In addition, mean sales prices were calculated by location. These calculations were further broken down by lot size. These results appear in Tables 7, 8, and 9. Table 6 presents a summary of these data by showing the percentage change in average prices that occurred between the three

Table 7

AVERAGE PRICES BY LOT SIZE AND LOCATION
January 1, 1955 to November 30, 1958*

	Mean Price ($)	Number of Properties in Sample		Standard Deviation ($)
LOT SIZE LESS THAN 5000 SQ.FT.				
Non-Control Group				
Rezoned lots	9473.53	34 } 96		2116.27
Non-rezoned lots	9884.27	62 }		3320.25
Ring 1	9385.00	10		1853.51
2	9510.41	24		2253.15
3	11275.00	12		2623.36
4	10415.38	13 } 96		4179.67
5	9444.73	19		2889.91
6	8254.54	11		3108.97
7	10267.86	7		3636.81
Control Group				
All lots (not rezoned)	10831.21	28		2537.21
Ring 1	10892.59	17		2500.53
2	9500.00	1 } 28		0.00
3	0.00	0 }		0.00
4	10860.00	10		2826.93
LOT SIZE GREATER THAN OR EQUAL TO 5000 SQ.FT.				
Non-Control Group				
Rezoned lots	14064.70	17 } 126		3932.10
Non-rezoned lots .	13844.04	109 }		3351.01
Ring 1	13642.86	7		5029.52
2	14360.00	10		3222.98
3	13842.86	14		2759.51
4	13420.00	15 } 126		3665.70
5	13536.11	18		3570.37
6	12618.52	27		2221.78
7	15130.00	35		3748.59
Control Group				
All lots (not rezoned)	13525.80	31		5110.38
Ring 1	15700.00	1		0.00
2	10475.00	2 } 31		671.81
3	11588.46	13 }		1702.94
4	15466.66	15		6652.56

Note: * Period 1

periods of study. From this table it can be seen that between Period 1 and Period 2 smaller non-rezoned lots increased at greater rates on average (23.2 per cent) than did rezoned lots (6.8 per cent). The same pattern was apparent in larger lots: 15.8 per cent for the non-rezoned compared to -4.6 per cent for the rezoned. Thus, anticipation of the zoning change as evidenced by the rezoning study appears to have had little

Table 8

AVERAGE PRICES BY LOT SIZE AND LOCATION
December 1, 1958 to June 30, 1961*

	Mean Price ($)	Number of Properties in Sample		Standard Deviation ($)
LOT SIZE LESS THAN 5000 SQ.FT.				
Non–Control Group				
Rezoned lots	10114.29	7	} 32	2888.13
Non-rezoned lots	12178.00	25		3647.65
Ring 1	11250.00	2		1767.76
2	9660.00	5		3290.59
3	15037.50	4		3492.22
4	12875.00	4	} 32	3604.03
5	11875.00	8		4077.02
6	9800.00	6		2915.47
7	13000.00	3		2605.75
Control Group				
All lots (not rezoned)	13375.00	4		5186.11
Ring 1	13166.66	3		6331.13
2	0.00	0	} 4	0.00
3	0.00	0		0.00
4	14000.00	1		0.00
LOT SIZE GREATER THAN OR EQUAL TO 5000 SQ.FT.				
Non–Control Group				
Rezoned lots	13416.66	12	} 65	2952.90
Non-rezoned lots	16029.24	53		4119.72
Ring 1	12200.00	5		4009.36
2	14285.71	7		1776.15
3	15655.55	9		2435.72
4	15383.33	6	} 65	4525.66
5	16643.75	8		2152.46
6	14296.66	15		3246.45
7	17916.66	15		5653.43
Control Group				
All lots (not rezoned)	14174.38	16		3567.08
Ring 1	17250.00	2		3323.38
2	11600.00	2	} 16	424.23
3	13750.00	7		2523.03
4	14568.00	5		5177.65

Note: * Period 2

impact on average sale prices between the periods. More-over, no evidence of registered options against property was uncovered. Thus, there was no unequivocal indication of speculative activity. It was impossible to rule this out entirely, however, as there appeared to be a disproportionate number of sales to non-residents.

Table 9

AVERAGE PRICES BY LOT SIZE AND LOCATION
July 1, 1961 to March 31, 1963*

	Mean Price ($)	Number of Properties in Sample		Standard Deviation ($)
LOT SIZE LESS THAN 5000 SQ.FT.				
Non-Control Group				
Rezoned lots	12217.78	9	} 30	2473.41
Non-rezoned lots	12091.66	21		4367.25
Ring 1	12786.66	3		1194.33
2	11933.33	6		2987.76
3	14087.50	4		1442.41
4	8700.00	6	} 30	2611.51
5	12562.50	6		4491.47
6	13300.00	2		11313.70
7	14466.66	3		1750.23
Control Group				
All lots (not rezoned)	11022.22	9		2159.99
Ring 1	10330.00	5		2125.91
2	11216.66	3	} 9	2052.03
3	0.00	0		0.00
4	13900.00	1		0.00
LOT SIZE GREATER THAN OR EQUAL TO 5000 SQ.FT.				
Non-Control Group				
Rezoned lots	22181.50	10	} 40	5708.00
Non-rezoned lots	14396.66	30		3248.33
Ring 1	18238.00	5		3579.83
2	26125.00	5		4649.19
3	12000.00	1		0.00
4	14280.00	5	} 40	2066.57
5	13300.00	10		2639.86
6	14760.00	5		4121.64
7	15744.44	9		3927.50
Control Group				
All lots (not rezoned)	14260.00	15		4852.61
Ring 1	0.00	0		0.00
2	12500.00	1	} 15	0.00
3	12010.00	5		2019.39
4	15705.55	9		5767.82

Note: * Period 3

Table 10
ECONOMIC INDICATORS, 1955-1963

Year	Per Capita Personal Income ($) Canada	B.C.	Housing Starts (Units) Canada	B.C.	Bond Yields (Per Cent) Federal	Mortgage Interest Rates (Per Cent)	GNE Price Deflator (1951=100)	Unemployment Rate (Per Cent) Canada	B.C.	New NHA House Price ($) Canada Avg.
1955	1355	1671	97,386	10,848	3.45	5.87	89.7	4.4	3.8	12,597
56	1463	1774	87,309	10,468	3.94	6.24	93.0	3.4	2.8	13,548
57	1515	1841	84,875	9,702	3.80	6.85	95.0	4.6	5.0	14,044
58	1560	1811	121,695	14,953	4.62	6.79	96.3	7.0	8.6	14,267
59	1608	1881	105,991	11,875	5.49	6.97	98.3	6.0	6.5	14,462
1960	1656	1909	76,687	6,442	5.31	7.17	99.5	7.0	8.5	14,273
61	1651	1898	92,741	7,760	4.95	7.00	100.0	7.1	8.5	14,463
62	1764	1975	96,598	9,665	5.12	6.97	101.4	5.9	6.6	14,684
63	1840	2065	120,950	12,559	5.17	6.97	103.2	5.5	6.4	15,068

Year	Unemployment (Thousands) Canada	B.C.	Employment (Thousands) Canada	B.C.	Residential Construction** ($ Millions) Canada	B.C.	Average New NHA House Price ($)	Trade ($ Millions) Canada	B.C.
1955	245	18	5364	462	1397	168	12,841	13,473	1447
56	197	14	5585	489	1547	173	13,854	14,774	1640
57	278	27	5731	509	1430	174	14,278	15,423	1683
58	432	47	5706	501	1782	211	14,479	16,139	1706
59	372	36	5870	521	1752	225	14,729	17,087	1793
1960	446	48	5965	516	1456	174	14,639	17,391	1755
61	466	49	6055	527	1467	149	14,888	17,752	1761
62	390	39	6225	551	1587	162	15,233	16,073	1604
63	374	39	6375	571	1713	208	15,682	17,137	1751

Notes: * Centers over 5,000 inhabitants
 ** Includes new construction and repairs

Sources: 1) Housing Data, CMHC
 2) Macroeconomic Data, Statistics Canada

The situation changes considerably, however, after the rezoning. Between Periods 2 and 3 (e.g., before and after the rezoning), one observes that smaller rezoned properties (20.8 per cent) greatly outpaced the non-rezoned ones (-0.7 per cent); this phenomena was again independent of lot size. Larger lots appreciated more rapidly, however, as is to be expected since larger land parcels entail fewer transactions in the land assembly process. The increase in rezoned lot prices is particularly dramatic since the non-rezoned properties were experiencing significant declines during the period consistent with general economic recession during the early 1960s (see Table 10, which shows per capita income, housing starts, and retail trade all remaining below their 1959 levels until 1963).

Armed with this information one can now return to the questions posed at the outset. First, zoning does have a significant impact on land use and value. In the case at hand, rezoned properties appreciated greatly in value relative to non-rezoned properties. On average, over the study period, rezoned properties increased in price by roughly 40 per cent compared with the roughly 5 per cent increase recorded by non-rezoned properties. Second, the effects were limited spatially to rezoned areas.

It seems clear that rezoning does matter in terms of increasing the value of the affected properties. Furthermore, the evidence shows that zoning has no appreciable impact on the values of adjacent non-rezoned properties (the properties in rings 3 to 7 changed in value at approximately the same rate as did the control area properties which were situated in Kerrisdale, a significant distance away). This impression that rezoning *does not* adversely affect surrounding property values is strengthened by a visual inspection of the rezoned area and the remaining single family homes immediately adjacent to it. The following photographs are numbered and can be identified on Map 3. Essentially, photographs 1 and 2 give some idea about the relationship between the rezoned area (high rise towers) and the existing commercial area along West 41st Avenue between Yew and Larch Streets. Photographs 3 and 4 depict the high rise and low rise multi family housing built as a result of the rezoning. Lastly, photographs 5 through 8 represent the remaining single family zone and place it in its context adjacent to the rezoned area. No blight has resulted from the rezoning, and the area is still a solid and sought-after single family area.

1

41st Avenue in Kerrisdale

2

3

The apartment zone in Kerrisdale

4

5

Single-family homes adjacent to apartments on Larch Street

6

7

Larch and 39th in Kerrisdale: single and multi-family zones

8

In summary, rezoning has had a very significant impact on the value of the rezoned properties. It has not, however, adversely affected the value of the remaining neighboring single family zone, nor has it hurt the area from an aesthetic point of view. Turning to the speculation question, we can see from the above that rezoned properties did increase significantly, relative to those that were not rezoned. Speculation was encouraged by the presence of the possibility of a zoning change. Analysis of the pattern of options registered and of sales to non-resident owners reveals that these indicators of speculative activity declined with distance from the rezoned area and were greatest in the rezoned rings, though the data were limited, and strong conclusions cannot be drawn on the question of speculation.

It appears, therefore, that the presence of zoning (and more specifically the possibility of changes in zoning) created a speculative environment within which investors/speculators were encouraged to move into the area to "bet" on the likelihood of zoning alterations. Such a finding is really not surprising. It has been observed in foreign exchange markets where so-called "fixed exchange rates" (e.g., tying a currency such as the Canadian dollar to another currency such as the pound and then using central bank reserves to maintain this fixed rate of exchange) tended to be destabilizing. The present system of flexible exchange rates (the so-called floating rate) which Canada has been following since 1970 appears to have allowed the Canadian dollar to absorb speculative and transaction demands by foreign exchange traders. There is an analogy to a kind of "floating zone" where speculative as well as "transactions demands" (e.g., user-dominated demands) for real property can be absorbed without the rigidity of the fixed uses prescribed by zoning.

Summary of empirical findings for Vancouver

1. Zoning changes do lead to changes in real property values; however, these changes are not always predictable. A number of rezonings that *a priori* would have been classed as upzonings to higher uses led to a decline in property values.

2. Changing zoning from a lower use (RS-1) to a higher and supposedly incompatible use (RM-3) led to increases in relative values for rezoned properties in Kerrisdale.

3. This rezoning also promoted some speculative activity in anticipation of the rezoning and higher real property

values, although this finding needs further investigation.

4. An examination of house price changes in adjacent areas and control groups showed no measurable negative external effects from the rezoning. Adjacent areas appreciated in value at the same rates as places farther away. A physical inspection of the area today, some seventeen years later, shows the single family district to be healthy and well maintained.

5. These findings are consistent with the other empirical studies reviewed earlier in this volume and lend further support to the rising criticism of zoning as virtually the sole land use and development control in common use in North America.

Some qualifications, extensions, and implications

A number of caveats should be registered. The data appear reasonable, as Tunnicliffe established by cross-matching of Assessor's records. Additional information would be desirable, however, to fully uncover the mechanism of price change. Most importantly, more data are needed about the houses described in the sample. Much of the variation observed in sale prices could be the result of different attributes of the particular houses. Dividing the transactions into properties of less and greater than 5,000 square feet accounts for only some of this variation. It was impossible, however, to obtain more detailed, reliable, and relevant information about the houses.

The study should be extended up to the present to test for the presence of externalities in areas close to the rezoned sectors. Also, in this vein, parallel studies should be attempted elsewhere to see if these findings are specific to the Vancouver region with its unique topography or if they are more broadly applicable to urban real property markets generally.

The foregoing implies that some of the stated objectives of zoning appear to be founded on improper assumptions about real property markets. More specifically, there appear to be only minimal (and usually unmeasurable) external effects. The stability of neighborhoods that zoning seeks to protect thus appears to be endangered by the rezoning that is part and parcel of the zoning by-laws in the first place.

Notes

1   Kenneth W. Tunnicliffe, "The Effect of Rezonings on Property Values," p. 3.

CHAPTER SIX
The Future and Relevance of Zoning —Suggested Reforms and Alternatives

CHAPTER SIX
The Future and Relevance of Zoning –Suggested Reforms and Alternatives

I. A LAND USE CONTROL TYPOLOGY

It is now appropriate to look beyond zoning in its narrowest sense to land use controls more broadly conceived. The following typology seems to be a convenient way to organize and summarize:

	Positive	Negative	
		(zoning)	Direct
			Indirect

We have been focusing our attention on only one of the four possible boxes: negative direct control through zoning. The ensuing discussion elaborates on this typology, by looking at negative controls in British Columbia as an example. Following this, we explore the idea of positive land use controls but find that such zoning, while prevalent, is never viewed as a control.

The British Columbia case is typical. Under Section 92 of the *British North America Act* of 1867, questions relating to real property and to municipalities are the exclusive responsibility of the provinces. Accordingly, every province has created cities under its mandate and has passed on to cities the responsibility for regulating land use and urban development. Some provinces, such as Ontario, British Columbia, and Alberta have seen fit to create other levels of government to control development both inside and outside cities.

Ontario has been most aggressive in this field, creating both a variety of regional governments and the Ontario Municipal Board. The Ontario cabinet still reserves the right to review a range of land use decisions, so in that province controls range from local municipal governments up through regional governments, the Ontario Municipal Board, and then the provincial cabinet.

Similarly, in Alberta control derives from the *Planning Act* and also from the provincial cabinet's ability to regulate annexation. Most decisions are delegated to municipalities and to the regional planning districts which span roughly half the province. Alberta has long been a leader and innovator and has pioneered in bringing development permits from the United Kingdom to North America.

While the ten provinces apply their mandate to administer cities quite differently, the general characteristics of municipal/provincial sharing of regulation of land uses are sufficiently similar to those in British Columbia to allow us to use it as a generic case.

II. NEGATIVE LAND USE CONTROLS

Direct land use controls

The principal means of controlling land use in British Columbia derive from the *Municipal Act*. This provides for the creation of zoning by-laws in each municipality along with the necessary implementation procedures. The land use contract is also specified in the act along with the rules for its implementation. It establishes the system of regional districts and allocates responsibilities to them. Left to the municipalities are the administrative procedures for carrying out the provisions of the act as well as the setting of fees, charges, etc.

Direct control is also exercised through the *Land Commission Act* which established the B.C. Land Commission to create agricultural reserves from land suited to such purposes. The Commission has the right to designate such lands as agricultural, and is also charged with hearing requests for removal of lands from the reserve. By directing the use of this type of land, particularly in the Vancouver and Victoria regions, the *Land Commission Act* has affected the supply of urbanizable land and represents a significant new kind of control.

Other forms of direct control include the *Limited Access Highways Act*, wherein any land development or rezoning by a municipality or regional district within one-half mile of a limited access highway must be approved in advance by the highways department. Requiring subdivisions to be connected to trunk sewers, given certain density and locational conditions (basically if they are small lot sub-divisions in urban areas) is another direct control that is provided for under the provincial *Health Act*. Crown owner-ship provides for another means of development control which can be viewed in both modes. It is direct since the province (or municipalities) through the ownership of land obviously have the greatest leeway in restricting its use. It can also be used as an indirect control when the government chooses to influence the market through the sale, lease, or development of its holdings. In British Columbia, the provin-cial government is by far the largest landowner and directly holds nearly 95 per cent of the land. This would give it great flexibility in regulating development via the market, should it choose to do so. A similar situation holds for the other provinces as can be seen from Table 11.

Indirect controls

There are a large number of government policies which fundamentally affect urban land markets, and as an indirect result provide policies for land use control. The relationship between transportation accessibility and land value is well known. Eased access to an area will have the effect of raising land values, all other things remaining constant, for it provides the site with a wider potential market and makes it more attractive. This shows itself in increased land values. Similar influences can be exerted by government through the location of sewer and water trunks, schools, parks, hydro facilities, and, in general, through the provision of amenities in a neighborhood. The provincial and local governments have a large number of tools at their disposal to affectuate policies such as those outlined above. Such programs do

Table 11
TOTAL AREA CLASSIFIED BY TENURE, 1976 (km²)

Item	Province or Territory												CANADA
	NFLD	PEI	NS	NB	QUE	ONT	MAN	SASK	ALTA	BC	YT	NWT	
Federal Crown lands other than national parks, Indian reserves, and forest experiment stations	440	16	181	1,489	1,295[1]	1,158	259	5,452	2,896[5]	904	513,193	3,340,849	3,868,132
National parks	2,339	21	1,331	433	790	1,922	2,978	3,875	54,084	4,690	22,015	35,690	130,168
Indian Reserves	-	8	114	168	4,077[2]	6,703	2,383	5,688	6,566	3,390	5	135	29,237
Federal forest experiment stations	-	-	-	91	28	103		-	155	-	-	-	377[6]
Privately owned land or land in process of alienation from the Crown	17,788	4,944	37,438	39,754	112,664	119,023	138,008[†]	247,662	181,925	55,040	168	72	795,800[6]
Provincial or territorial area other than provincial parks and provincial forests[3]	382,842	435	2,652	28,495	1,210,799	891,261	482,204[4]	34,758	63,525[7]	539,280	943	2,937	3,621,560
Provincial parks	805	31	109	215	194,249	48,412	10,230	4,944	7,700	41,629	-	-	308,187
Provincial forests	303	202	13,665	2,792	16,778	-	14,025	349,521	344,334[8]	303,663	-	-	1,084,669
Total area	404,517	5,657	55,490	73,437	1,540,680	1,068,582	650,087	651,900	661,185	948,596	536,324	3,379,683	9,976,138
Per centage of total area that is privately owned	4.4%	87.4%	67.5%	54.1%	7.3%	11.1%	21.2%	38.0%	27.5%	5.8%	0.03%	0.002%	8.0%

Notes:
1. Includes Gatineau Park (356.1 km²) and Quebec Battlefields Park (0.93 km²) which are under federal jurisdiction but are not technically national parks.
2. Includes increase awarded by the James Bay Agreement.
3. Includes freshwater area.
4. Includes only those provincial lands held under Crown Lands Act, of which 7,280 km² are under lease.
5. Excludes Department of National Defence agreement areas.
6. Excludes area for Manitoba (federal forest experiment stations are combined with privately owned land or land in process of alienation from the Crown, for that province).
7. Includes lands held by the federal government under agreement with Alberta (one national defence area and one agriculture experiment station).
8. Includes Department of National Defence agreement area.

Source: Canada Year Book 1978-79, Statistics Canada

†Editor's Note: This figure represents the total land in Manitoba in federal forest experiment stations and privately owned land in process of alienation from the Crown.

influence the relative attractiveness of sites served by them and thus can act as a stimulant to private investment in these areas, or can act to change the kind of investment that the private sector is making in the area (from industrial to residential/commercial as is likely to be the case in False Creek, Vancouver; in the St. Lawrence Market area of Toronto; and in Palmer Square, Calgary).

Just as governments can positively affect land markets, so can they act as a deterrent to investment. As a general rule, government policies that lower returns to developers will discourage urban investment. Thus, removing the tax shelter provisions in the federal *Income Tax Act* did have a noticeable impact on returns and, therefore, on the attractiveness of real estate as an investment. A similar example is provided by the *Landlord and Tenant Act* which has imposed rent control on residential rental properties. The rigidity of such controls has lowered the return to developers during a period of rapid inflation and thus, discouraged investors from this kind of accommodation.

III. POSITIVE CONTROLS

Direct positive controls are impractical

It is not feasible to require landowners to build on vacant land. As was seen in the case of the area near East 43rd Avenue and Fraser Street, rezoning to a higher density does not necessarily encourage development. Thus, direct positive controls, short of ordering landowners to develop land with specific types of structures, is not possible in the private market. It is entirely possible, however, for the government to "positively" control development through the direct placement of desired structures such as public buildings, offices, parks, etc. More generally though, public sector investment will work as an indirect "control" (inducement).

Indirect controls can be a positive influence

These are exercised by the authorities every time they make a decision to provide infrastructure and amenities. In the case of Houston, while governments did not control land use through zoning, the patterns of land use were certainly influenced by the placement of sewers, water mains, and most importantly, freeways and major arterial streets and car parks. In a completely analogous manner, the location of community centers, swimming pools, skating rinks, parks, and other amenity packages provides significant inducement to help create the kinds of urban development deemed socially desirable. Rail relocation schemes in Ottawa and Saskatoon also do a great deal to change the environment in directions favored by the planning authorities. Such positive but indirect "controls" should be given prominent attention for guiding urban development as they allow for significant flexibility and responsiveness.

IV.   SUGGESTED ALTERNATIVES: LOOKING FOR OTHER APPROACHES TO CONTROL LAND USE

Two extreme positions exist from which we can search for alternatives: no zoning or land use controls at all, or total predetermined and immutable delineation of land uses. In other words, the whole idea behind zoning is inappropriate and deserves to be chucked out, or the idea was sound but we failed to apply it rigorously enough.

As with most real world policy issues, the search should perhaps be confined to the area lying within these extreme points. As a general rule, movements toward the non-zoning extreme are in our opinion desirable. The exact nature and extent of this movement from our present position needs to be firmly rooted in local values, perceptions, and conditions. The land use contract system used in British Columbia until 1977 is an interesting example of an essentially "non-zoning state" which retains control of land use and the fiscal and environmental impacts of urban development. (That system has been replaced by a development permit system that is potentially more general still, but the new system is too new to present us with any usable experience upon which to comment.)

The development permit system has been in long use in the United Kingdom. In its most flexible form (and the one we would advocate) it allows developers and redevelopers to come forward with specific proposals that are each evaluated on their merits. Once again, there is no zoning in the traditional sense, but there are still controls.

Taking this system one step further would find us with no zoning, but with a well-defined and carefully proscribed control process where the various decision points and variables are clearly specified in the law or in the regulations governing the approval process. So long as the decision rules are clearly enunciated, and so long as the approval process is equally well-defined, then a development permit system could function smoothly and allow for innovation and quality in land use and urban development without needless and often avoidable delays. It should be noted that even in Houston there is a well-defined subdivision and permit approval process that governs urban development, though land use is left entirely up to the developer's discretion. In essence, Houston functions without zoning of land use controls, but within a well-defined and well-publicized development approval process. As such, it represents something less than the totally unfettered development procedure which sketches out our extreme position.

Another approach toward a more flexible set of guidelines is to make judicious use of spot rezoning. Spot zoning (and rezoning) is the ultimate bane of the zoner's existence. It is viewed as a compromise of the basic principles of zoning and land use controls and, therefore, morally reprehensible and beyond the realm of serious consideration. But it has several advantages. By rezoning individual parcels as interesting and high quality development proposals come forward, we allow for innovation and experimentation, while moderating the negative effects that accompany unsuccessful attempts. Innovation is a risky business and to minimize or, more accurately, to properly contain the risk, rezoning individual parcels allows for small-scale experiments which will be minimally disruptive to surrounding properties and neighborhoods. The public, thus, receives the benefit of the experiment, and allows the developer/innovator to bear most of the risk. Large-scale rezoning, although it is acceptable to planners, greatly increases societal risk and can be counterproductive, as has been noted previously. The possibility of spot rezoning also erodes the quasi-monopoly position that zoning bestows on property owners and allows for competition among innovators. It, thus, promotes innovation and experimentation, all the while containing the experiment within well-defined spatial boundaries so that the entrepreneur, not the society or the neighborhood, suffers if the experiment proves unsuccessful.

In addition to these direct forms of land use control, a range of indirect controls also exists. Once again, the City of Houston uses infrastructure placement as a key ingredient in its development and planning policy. By carefully locating and timing the placement of sewers, waterlines, streets, and other public services, Houston does in fact exercise significant control over urban development, albeit indirectly. As a general rule, the careful placement of public investment can be as important and effective in guiding urban development as rigid negative direct controls such as zoning have been, without the high cost in time, bureaucracy, and homogeneity which has gone hand in hand with such traditional controls.

V.   SOME QUESTIONS TO PONDER

In concluding this brief look at land use controls it is appropriate to pose a number of questions for discussion purposes.   The questions provide a framework for drawing conclusions that permit the reader to make his or her own assessment.

The material in this monograph strongly suggests that we question existing land use controls and any future controls and ask whether they meet a number of criteria:

1) Does zoning introduce greater uncertainty into urban land markets than would prevail in its absence?

2) Does the individual investor face more or less uncertainty as a result of the use of zoning to control land use?

3) Are more flexible but administratively more involved approaches such as development permits and land use contracts preferable?

4) Might planned unit developments (PUDs) be the answer?

5) Is flexibility a desirable attribute of land use controls?

6) Who should decide how land is used?
   a) Politicians?
   b) Citizen groups and public participation?
   c) Interest groups such as Boards of Trade and developers?
   d) Urban technicians such as planners, engineers, and economists?

7) Should we retain our present views toward property rights, and the rights of the individual to develop property to its highest and best use, or should we adopt a philosophy similar to that of the *Uthwatt Report* and see all increments in value and use as flowing to and from the public?   In short, should there be a private real property market at all?   Or, should there be totally unfettered urban development without any form of zoning, as in Houston?

VI. SUMMING UP AND CONCLUDING

Zoning has not worked very well. The externalities that it is designed to ameliorate have been shown to be minimal or non-existent. The windfall profits it was intended to control have been instead *guaranteed* as a result of the quasi-monopoly bestowed on parcels capable of being used at higher uses, while holding surrounding and competing parcels at lower uses. The maintenance of single family neighborhoods by zoning statutes is also questionable: by keeping land and buildings in the same use over time, zoning can promote neighborhood decay and speed the demise of the single family neighborhood. Zoning is a rigid control, and is likely to fracture during times of change in consumer tastes, neighborhood demographic structure, urban growth, and transportation and building technologies. Finally, contrary to its intended purpose as a mitigator of speculative activity, zoning (and the anticipation of changes in zoning that goes with it) promotes speculation and non-resident ownership.

The record is quite clear and unambiguous: zoning has been far less successful than intended. Unfortunately, the alternatives are not as clear-cut. Zoning as a system of regulating land uses in urban areas has evolved over the past half-century and is now almost as diverse as it is ubiquitous. Suggestions that it can be scrapped and immediately replaced by less obtrusive and hopefully more effective policies are likely to be as unsuccessful in their own right as zoning has been. The Houston example of non-zoning works - in Houston. Imposing such a system across the rest of North America would represent a major, and probably disastrous, change from present practice. What is needed is a range of alternatives that can be implemented simultaneously and which over time can come to replace the rigidity and ineffectiveness of zoning with more malleable, sensitive, and appropriate controls. These should be selective enough to achieve quite well-defined and specific goals. They should not try to accomplish numerous goals simultaneously and fail to attain any one of them particularly well.

The gradual phasing in of selective spot-zones to accommodate high quality innovative development is a move in the direction advocated here. More flexible mixed-use zones would also begin to overcome the rigidities and dullness of traditional single-use zones. Floating zones that allow a range of developments within broad guidelines would also be a constructive step toward the dezoning of land use controls.

In such zones we might allow housing of various types to be constructed, along with the necessary retail and commercial supporting activities, as long as certain guidelines, perhaps with respect to building scale and mix, could be met. Land use contracts (e.g., various forms of zoning for sale) also represent a step toward greater flexibility and responsiveness.

Our work, and that of others, has shown zoning to be ineffective and, at times, even counterproductive. It needs to be replaced. Care must be taken that in the transition to more flexible systems of land use control, greater problems than those currently caused by zoning are assiduously avoided where possible. There should be a gradual evolution of more sensitive and flexible means of influencing the quality and course of urban development. The more willing we are to experiment with alternatives that suit local needs and values, the more likely are we to find the appropriate mix of policies that will ensure high quality urban development, consistent with community and larger societal objectives, and which will be economically viable as well. An exciting future lies ahead if we are willing to devote the time and creativity to the task, not just as developers, planners, or other variants of urban experts, but as informed citizens.

It is as citizens that we must ultimately come to grips with the questions that zoning has largely dealt with unsuccessfully. The present volume is directed toward providing citizens with the current state of knowledge on the subject of zoning so that they may be informed and, thus, influence policy based on knowledge, not only on narrowly and often ill-conceived perceptions of "the facts." Armed with more knowledge, we can forge new experiments to create new knowledge and urban environments appropriate to our values, needs, and resources.

APPENDIX
A Graphical Analysis
of Land Use Zoning
by David E. Baxter

APPENDIX
A Graphical Analysis of Land Use Zoning by David E. Baxter

I.   INTRODUCTION

Zoning is the specification, in a statute or by-law, of the legally permitted use of land parcels. The main purpose of this appendix is to look at the effects of such government regulation on the operation of land markets.

This ordinance directly affects both the price and amount of land available for each prescribed activity. Further affected are the supply of goods and services produced by land-using activities.   Although generally ignored, zoning thus influences not only the value of land, but also the price of consumer commodities.

A glance at a two-dimensional map often gives the impression that a neat and tidy spatial ordering of land will result from zoning. This is perhaps a comfort to those who share the belief that chaos would reign without public land use controls. Economist Richard Muth has noted that a chaos theory of unregulated land markets is common even amongst scholars.   In *Cities and Housing*,[1]   however, Muth demonstrates the inappropriateness of such chaos theories, and concludes:

Contrary to the belief of many housing and urban land economists, the theoretical and empirical techniques of modern economic analysis yield highly fruitful results when applied to housing and urban land markets, provided that, as in any applied field of economics, account is taken of a few special features of these markets. Contrary to the implications of the crude form of the chaos hypothesis, the distribution of population within cities and the quality of their housing exhibit strong regularities and are highly predictable. Contrary to the more sophisticated version of the chaos hypothesis, our urban problems arise for reasons almost totally unrelated to external economies, market imperfections and the lack of planning and governmental control. Problems certainly do exist in urban areas, but the real nature of these problems is not well understood. Many current governmental programs in the housing and urban fields for this reason are at best of little value and may do real harm.

The pattern of land uses in the absence of zoning may differ to some extent from those which would exist with such controls - although the findings of Siegan[2] suggest that the differences may not be as significant as proponents of the chaos theory would suggest. Further, the placement of productive activity which emerges from the market process is orderly, logical, and predictable - but only from an economic and cost-saving perspective. This is not always appreciated by zoning professionals who are more spatially oriented, and concerned with two-dimensional neatness and tidiness.

One of the sources of misunderstanding about the operation of the land market stems from the fact that many people experience the process of change in land use only in the context of discrete, and often dramatic, alterations in the use of single specific properties. The focus on the change in individual trees may lead to an obscured vision of the broader pattern of evolution in the entire forest.

II. CHARACTERISTICS AND ATTRIBUTES OF LAND

Improvement and services

Land is seldom of any value without on- or off-site modification to make it usable. Real estate, real property, and improved or developed land are essentially synonymous terms referring to the erection of structures, alteration of topography, and connection to community infrastructure and services. Land, once developed, provides an environment - shelter, support, and climate - for human activities.

These environmental (or real property) services are used together with other resources in the creation of goods and services. Thus, the value of occupying or otherwise using a parcel of real property depends upon its potential to contribute to the production of commodities. Even improved land is worthless unless some user places a value on the services the property is capable of providing.

Immobility

The outstanding characteristic of real estate is its immobility. "Land" is simply a shorthand phrase used to refer to specific portions of the surface of the earth which, of course, cannot be moved from one location to another. Although the non-land resources used in development are mobile beforehand, once they are "attached" to the land, they take on some of the land's characteristic immobility. Only at great cost can even a small portion of the improvements be separated and moved to another location.

The immobility of land means that real property cannot be moved from one region to another where it might have a greater value. This is why real estate markets are local (or regional) markets, where value is determined by local supply and demand factors. The inventories of economically worthless, but physically usable, real estate in ghost towns provide mute testimony to the consequences of immobility on the operation of land markets.

Immobility also influences intraregional market operation. Since land is immobile, someone wishing to use the services of a specific property must travel there in order to do so: consumption or utilization of real property services must occur on site. The relative ease with which one property can be reached from another affects the utilization costs and, consequently, the relative value of its services to potential users. Location and transportation costs, thus, play fundamental roles in the market determination of values and uses.

The ease of movement of people and goods between spatially separate parcels of improved land is of great importance in modern nations, for industrialization is fostered by and leads to specialization, with resulting economic interdependence. Specialization of activities leads to specialization of land use. The relative ease of movement between interdependent but spatially separate land-using activities becomes increasingly important. This explains the significance of location in the determination of land use and real estate values in urbanized and industrialized regions.

The immobility of land may also create "ownership externalities." An externality is generally said to exist where the costs and/or benefits of an economic activity are not fully borne by the concerned parties. For example, automobile drivers do not usually have to consider the costs of air pollution borne by other inhabitants of a region. In the case of real property, the use of one parcel of improved land may affect others, either beneficially or adversely. These external effects will be reflected in the capital values of the properties. If the use of one parcel is *changed*, adjacent owners may find the value of their property altered. Since real property is immobile, owners cannot move either toward or away from land-using activities which create external effects.

These effects are called "ownership externalities" since they will only be considered if affected properties are held under separate ownership. Under unified ownership, effects on adjacent parcels will be taken into account as decision makers will be faced with the full costs and benefits of their actions. Having noted that the immobility of real property creates the potential for such externalities, it must also be said that there is little evidence which indicates that these effects are, in fact, widespread.

Durability

In general, improvements to land are extremely durable. Consequently, real property has the physical capacity to be used continuously for decades or even centuries without major additions of capital after initial construction. The value of improved land changes because of economic, not physical, obsolescence. (Economic obsolescence is said to exist when the capital value of an alternative level of improvement exceeds the capital value of the current level of improvement by more than the costs of changing the improvements to the new use.)

The costs of land development, including the price paid are historical or sunk costs, and do not influence the value of the property. The value of the property is determined by its value to users (i.e., by demand) and not by its production or replacement costs. Again, ghost towns demonstrate that demand, not historical or current production costs, determines the value of improved land. The durability of improvements means that property may be developed under one set of market conditions, but will still be physically usable, at no new production cost, in markets where conditions were not foreseen initially.

New development and improvement of land reflects current expectations about future market conditions. Over time, as markets and expectations change, a heterogeneous stock of real estate develops. Many properties in this stock will not match the form of improvements and use that would occur if the entire stock could be replaced costlessly. However, their value in current use may be greater than the demolition value that would be realized if they were redeveloped. As conversion is not costless, and as the improvements do have some value, they will remain economically viable so long as the capital value of the property in its current use exceeds its demolition value. This indicates that the property is worth more in its current use than as an input to redevelopment.

III. DETERMINANTS OF LAND USE PATTERNS: A GRAPHICAL MODEL

Introduction

In order to discuss the effects of zoning, it is necessary to first review the economic processes which affect the use of improved land. The model presented in this section is derived from the theory of the operation of land markets as presented in the literature of urban land economics. The conceptual basis for the model may be traced back to the writings of Ricardo and von Thunen.[3] In the contemporary context, however, the writings of William Alonso,[4] particularly in *Location and Land Use*, have been generally[5] accepted as the conceptual basis for analysis of the economic factors which determine land use. Alonso concentrates upon location, transportation costs, and land uses.

The model has been modified to take into account the costs and durability of improvements, as well as accessibility. It is simplified and intended to elucidate the general effects of the regulation of land use, not the specific characteristics of any one region or form of land use regulation. A hypothetical agricultural land market is presented, but the underlying principles apply equally to the urban environment as well.

107

Basic principles - a single land use

The utilization of resources is ultimately derived from the conditions which prevail in the consumer (or final) market for goods and services. However, in responding to consumer demand, producers are constrained by the availability and prices of input factors (including transportation costs) and by the existing technology of production. The analysis of the operation of land markets, therefore, involves consideration of the characteristics of both consumer and intermediate markets.

The following assumptions are made:

1) a large agricultural region forms the hinterland for an urban area;
2) given current consumer demand, input prices, and agricultural technology, only wheat is grown in the region;
3) the wheat growing industry is comprised of a large number of independent farmers;
4) as this industry represents a very small portion of all non-land inputs (e.g., capital, labor, machinery, etc.) changes in industry demand for these factors will have no effect on their price;
5) all farmers are tenants,[6] paying rent for the right to use the land for wheat growing;
6) all parcels of improved land are of equal productivity;
7) the costs of transporting wheat increase with distance from the urban area (the marketplace);
8) costs of transporting any non-land inputs to production are negligible, and, hence, may be considered to be included in the costs of transporting wheat. All farmers, therefore, face the same costs for non-land inputs;[7]
9) the market is in equilibrium (i.e., there are no expectations of, or current incentives to, change in production or consumption) both internally and with all other markets; and
10) all farmers face the same market price for wheat and costs for non-land inputs to production.

The market characteristics which will prevail in these circumstances are depicted in Figure Ia, and are analyzed in the remainder of this section. The wheat industry supply curve (Sw) will intersect the aggregate demand curve (Dw) at a market clearing price per bushel of wheat ($Pw) and level of production (Qw). This quantity is the result of the production decisions of all individual wheat farmers. During the process of market adjustment which leads up to this equilibrium state, farmers will have adjusted production to conform to expected market prices, the technologically feasible combinations of land and non-land inputs at each level of output, and the costs of transporting wheat to the market. This leads to a production level at each location which ensures producers of sufficient compensation and induces them to continue production. There are no "excess" profits (or losses) at equilibrium and, hence, no endogenous reason for further change.

Figures Ib and Ic depict the spatial pattern of prices and uses which will prevail with this initial equilibrium in the final market. Farmers will adjust their production and input to account for the difference in transportation costs that exists between sites, thereby underscoring the influence of land immobility. These differential costs are reflected in land rents. Very accessible locations are, in the absence of competition, more attractive, as such sites offer the potential for considerable savings in transportation costs. However, through competition for the right to use these accessible sites, the potential transportation savings are "bid away" into higher rents. Less accessible sites involve much higher transportation costs and, consequently, farmers will be willing to pay less for the right to use them. At equilibrium, the rents farmers pay will fully reflect the difference in transportation costs associated with using each site. The inverse relationship between transportation costs and rent paid for land as an input to the production of wheat is indicated by the decline as a function of increasing distance, of the bid rent curve ($Rw), shown on Figure Ib.

The differences in rent that result from competition for land, given the spatial difference in transportation costs, ensure that all farmers earn normal (but not excess) profits. These differences also affect how intensely each site is used. Rents reflect the value of the services provided by land in relation to wheat production. Given such a situation, farmers at highly accessible sites will attempt to economize on real property services by using a greater proportion of non-land inputs per unit of output. Fertilizer, labor, etc., will be used more intensively at highly accessible sites. Thus, land rents ensure that parcels close to market are used more intensely than those farther away. This brings about a more efficient utilization of resources: transport costs are minimized. Compared to a uniform distribution of crops, less input tonnage need be carried to the outlying districts and fewer outputs have to be brought into the city. This process, referred to as factor substitution, explains why the rent curve is depicted as a curved rather than a straight line - as rents fall, proportionately more land is used as an input to production.

The discussion thus far has concentrated on the process of establishing rents for *improved land*. This, however, is only part of the process by which land uses are determined. The fact that farmers would pay a positive rent for improved land is a necessary, but not a sufficient, factor in the determination of land uses. As land can be used in wheat production only if improved,† its value and the costs of land development will also play a role in land use.

The capital value of improved land is determined by calculating the present worth of periodic rent payments net of any variable costs. Thus, landowners subtract from the expected gross rental receipts in each future time period the costs expected to be incurred in the same period. This expected net cash flow, or net income, is discounted at the investor's minimum required return on capital to determine the present value (or investment value) of the property. This is the maximum amount an investor would pay for the right to receive such future expected rent payments. Thus, capital values of improved land are a function of rents (as indicated by the graph of capital values, $Cw, in Figure Ib).

A positive capital value (which derives from a positive net income) for improved land does not, however, imply that the land will be improved. Prior to improving their land for use, owners will subtract the associated capital costs ($CCw) from its capital value when improved. Only if the resulting "land residual" ($Lw) is positive (within distance d of the regional center on Figures Ib and Ic) will there exist an incentive to develop land. If this land residual is negative (as it is beyond distance d on Figures Ib and Ic), the value of the resources required to develop the property exceeds the value of the improved property, and a misallocation of resources (as well as a loss to the developer) would occur if improvement was carried out. A positive land residual, on the other hand, indicates that the value of the land, when improved, is greater than the cost of improvement: the opportunity of realizing the difference in value forms the incentive to

---

† Editor's Note: Improvement as explained above involves not only cleaning, grading, and draining or irrigating, but also involves off-site capital expenditure necessary to make the site accessible.

Figure I
A SINGLE LAND USE AT MARKET EQUILIBRIUM

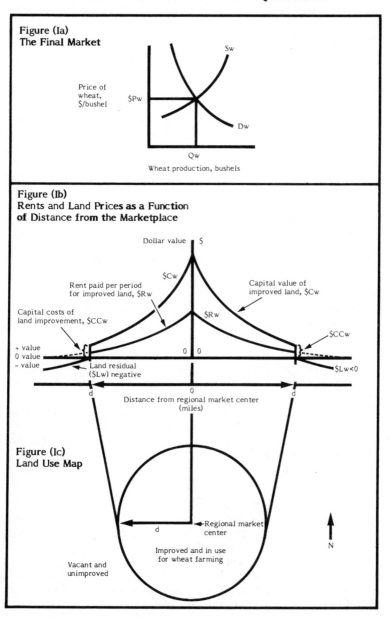

Figure (Ia)
The Final Market

Price of wheat, $/bushel

$Pw

Sw

Dw

Qw

Wheat production, bushels

Figure (Ib)
Rents and Land Prices as a Function of Distance from the Marketplace

Dollar value $

$Cw

Rent paid per period for improved land, $Rw

Capital value of improved land, $Cw

Capital costs of land improvement, $CCw

$Rw

$CCw

+ value
0 value
- value

Land residual ($Lw) negative

$Lw<0

d

0

d

Distance from regional market center (miles)

Figure (Ic)
Land Use Map

d

Regional market center

N

Improved and in use for wheat farming

Vacant and unimproved

111

development. Wherever the land residual is negative, the land will remain vacant and unimproved (as is shown in Figure Ic) even though the land would earn a positive rent if it was improved, as the value of improvement is less than its cost.

The basic model – land use competition

To evaluate the effects of zoning on the operation of land markets, it is necessary to take into account competition between alternative land use activities. Accordingly, a second agricultural activity - vegetable farming - is incorporated into the model. While the basic conclusions about market operation presented earlier remain unchanged, further dimensions may be characterized through this modification.

The conditions which characterize initial equilibrium in the two-land use model are depicted in Figure II. Figure IIa indicates the equilibrium conditions in the final markets where the initial market clearing prices of wheat ($\$Pw_1$ per bushel) and of vegetables ($\$Pv_1$ per bushel) are determined. Figure IIb depicts rents and land values as a function of distance and type of use. In developing this characterization, it was further assumed that:

11) the entire region was originally developed for wheat farming. As demand thresholds were passed, it became feasible to produce vegetables from within the region rather than importing them;

12) vegetable farmers are able to pay a higher rent than wheat farmers at highly accessible sites (i.e., $\$Rv_1 > \$Rw_1$ close to the common regional market center);

13) due to relatively higher transportation costs, wheat is able to support higher rents than vegetables at sites distant from the common regional market center (i.e., where $\$Rw_1 > \$Rv_1$); and

14) the capital costs of converting a wheat farm to a vegetable farm are positive (i.e., $\$CCwr > 0$).

At equilibrium, vegetable farming will only occur at those sites where the capital value of vegetable farms ($\$Cv$) exceeds the capital value of wheat farms ($\$Cw$) by an amount greater than or equal to the costs of converting ($\$Cwv$) a wheat farm to a vegetable farm (i.e., where $\$Cv - Cwv \geq \$Cw$). If such conditions do not exist, there is no incentive to convert to a vegetable farm even if its net rent (and, hence, capital value) is greater than that of the wheat

Figure II
INITIAL EQUILIBRIUM WITH TWO LAND USES

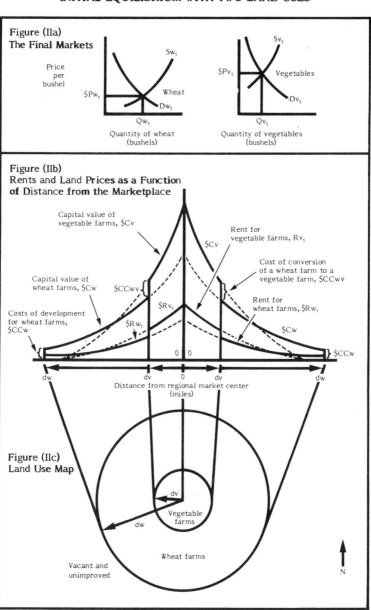

113

farm since the opportunity cost of the wheat farm *plus* the costs of conversion are greater than the benefits conversion would create.

Thus, vegetable farming will only occur within a distance of dv miles from the regional center (as is shown on Figures IIb and IIc), even though the vegetable farmers could pay more rent than wheat farmers beyond this distance.

An important conclusion to be drawn from this analysis is that rent-paying ability alone does not determine land use. For one activity to successfully compete for improved land, the net present value of its expected rental payments (the capital value of the land in the particular use) must exceed the capital value of the land in its current use by an amount equal to or greater than the costs of redevelopment and/or conversion. Only if conversion were costless and ownership costs associated with alternative land uses identical, would the rent and the capital value criteria lead to the same land use pattern.

IV. LAND USE AND ZONING:
A CONCEPTUAL ANALYSIS

Introduction

In this section, the model is used to evaluate the general effects of zoning. This is done by comparing land market adjustment to a change in consumer demand with and without this ordinance. Three types are considered: (a) "status quo" zoning, (b) "overzoning," and (c) "directional" zoning. While the examples presented are extremely simple, they, nevertheless, demonstrate the economic consequences of zoning.

The conditions depicted in Figure II relate to an equilibrium where there are no expectations of change in conditions in final or intermediate markets. In each of the four cases now considered, the market is assumed to be at this equilibrium initially; the final demand for vegetables is then assumed to undergo an unexpected increase. The process of market adjustment towards a new equilibrium is then described.

The unregulated response

There are three states in the process of market response to a change in final demand - the short (Figure III), intermediate (Figure IV), and long-run (Figure V) adjustments. In all cases, the increase in final demand for vegetables is shown as movement from Dv_1 to Dv_2 (Figures IIIa, IVa, and Va). In the short run, the increase in final demand must be, by definition,

Figure III
SHORT RUN RESPONSES

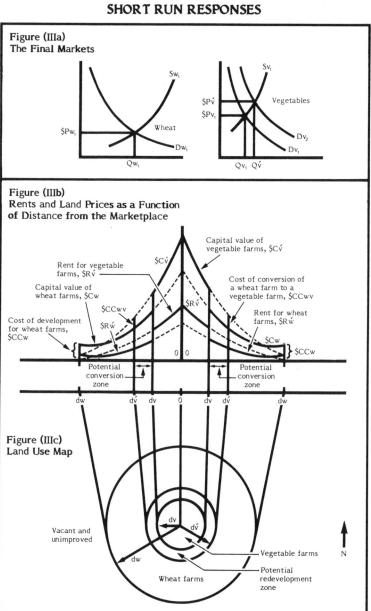

Figure (IIIa)
The Final Markets

Figure (IIIb)
Rents and Land Prices as a Function
of Distance from the Marketplace

Figure (IIIc)
Land Use Map

met entirely by more production from existing vegetable farms. Market prices (P\acute{v}$) and output (Q$\acute{v}$) are determined by the intersection of the initial industry supply curve (Sv$_1$) and the new final demand (Dv$_2$) in Figure IIIa. The surge in market prices (Pv_1$ to P\acute{v}$) will induce an increase in the intensity of use and, consequently, in the rental value (Rv_1$ in Figure IIb to R\acute{v}$ in Figure IIIb) of existing vegetable farms. The extent of the increased intensity will be dependent upon the technological constraints on the rise in production from existing vegetable farms.

The upswing in rental values of existing vegetable farms will result in a greater capital value. Owners of adjacent existing wheat farms in the ring lying between dv and d$\acute{v}$ miles (in Figure IIIc) from the regional market center will consider the feasibility of altering their land in order to make it suitable for vegetable farming. In doing so, they consider not the short-run rents (R\acute{v}$ in Figure IIIb) that will result from this increase, but rather the lower long-run rents that will pertain when market adjustment is completed (Rv_2$ as shown in Figure Vb). Parenthetically, failure to distinguish between short- and long-run rent changes has caused some investors serious problems resulting from the overbuilding that such shortsightedness induces. Landowners properly determine the development value of their land on the basis of its projected capital value when redeveloped for vegetable farming, minus the capital costs of such redevelopment. If this exceeds the value of the land in its current use, redevelopment can be profitable.

Assuming that redevelopment is feasible for some wheat farms, landowners will initiate the process. The market response during the intermediate or redevelopment stage is shown in Figure IV. The vegetable industry supply curve will shift outwards (Sv$_1$ to S$\acute{v}$) as the new farms expand the industry's productive capacity as is shown on Figure IVa. This will result in a decline in the market price (P\acute{v}$ to P\acute{\acute{v}}$), an increase in the quantity supplied to the market (Q$\acute{v}$ to Q$\acute{\acute{v}}$), and a reduction in the rent (R\acute{v}$ in Figure IIIb to R\acute{\acute{v}}$ in Figure IVb), and intensified use of existing vegetable farms (shown on Figure IVc).

However, these effects will also be reflected in the intermediate stage of the wheat market adjustment. The conversion of wheat to vegetable farms will result in a reduction in the size of the wheat-growing industry, and will be reflected in (a) a contraction of this industry's market supply curve (Sw$_1$ to S$\acute{w}$); (b) an increase in the market price

Figure IV
INTERMEDIATE RESPONSES

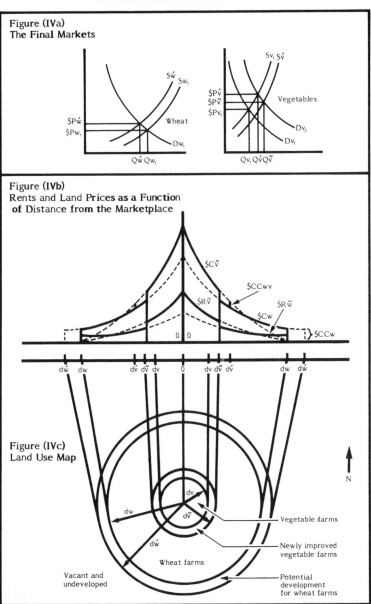

Figure (IVa)
The Final Markets

Figure (IVb)
Rents and Land Prices as a Function
of Distance from the Marketplace

Figure (IVc)
Land Use Map

117

of wheat ($\$Pw_1$ to $\$P\acute{w}$); and (c) a reduction in the quantity of wheat produced (Qw_1 to $Q\acute{w}$), as is shown on Figure IVa. Consequently, there will be an increase in the rent ($\$Rw_1$ in Figure IIIb to $R\acute{w}$ in Figure IVb) paid for existing wheat farms. This will be reflected in raised capital values, which will have two effects on landowners. First, the opportunity cost of existing wheat farms will increase, thereby reducing the amount of redevelopment to vegetable farms at the margin. Second, owners of vacant land adjacent to existing wheat farms (in the ring lying between dw and $d\acute{w}$ miles from the regional center in Figure IVc) may now find that the residual capital values warrant the development of wheat farming. Thus, the increase in final demand for vegetables may result in both redevelopment and new development.

The long-run adjustment is completed when an equilibrium state again exists, a situation where the relationships between capital values in both uses and the development and redevelopment costs leave no incentives for alteration of the physical characteristics of land in the region. Such a situation is shown in Figure V. The increase in demand for vegetables results ultimately in more vegetable farming land, additional vegetables, a change in the location of wheat farming, and a decrease in the market supply of wheat. Further, the rents paid for all improved land in the region have risen, a phenomenon known as the land ratchet effect. This ascent in land prices creates a situation where all land-using industries are, to one extent or another, cost generating: new equilibrium prices ($\$Pv_2$) are, therefore, shown as being slightly greater than they were initially ($\$Pv_1$ in Figure Va).

The regulated response: status quo zoning

Status quo zoning refers to controls which permit only the use which prevails when the by-law is implemented. The apparent intention is to preserve the existing land use pattern. Examples are the designation or zoning of farmlands for agricultural purposes (to prevent conversion to urban uses) and of single detached residential areas (to prevent redevelopment to other uses or higher density).

Clearly, status quo zoning will have an effect on the operation of land markets only if market conditions dictate a change in land use. The effects in these circumstances can be evaluated using the model presented in the preceding section. Assume that (a) prior to the increase in the demand for vegetables, all improved land was zoned for its prevailing

118

Figure V
FINAL EQUILIBRIUM

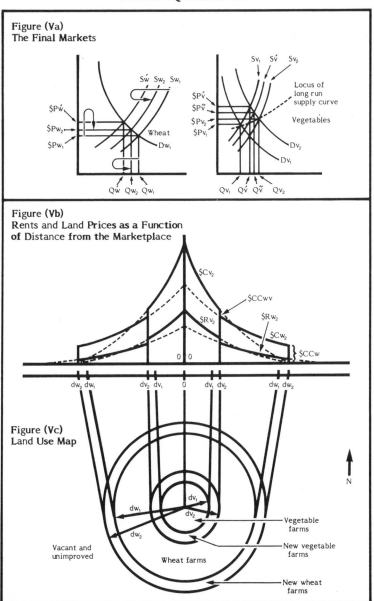

Figure (Va)
The Final Markets

Figure (Vb)
Rents and Land Prices as a Function
of Distance from the Marketplace

Figure (Vc)
Land Use Map

use, and (b) all unimproved land was not zoned and, therefore, could legally be improved for either use when economically feasible.

As conversion from wheat to vegetable farming is now prohibited, the additional consumer demand for vegetables can only be met through more output from existing vegetable farms.† Further, as no conversion can occur, the wheat industry is unaffected by the change in the demand for vegetables. Consequently, no improvement of previously vacant land for wheat farming will occur even though the zoning by-law permits this.

The long-run market response to the change in the demand for vegetables in the presence of status quo zoning is identical to the short-run response that will occur in the absence of this law (Figure III). Thus, zoning acts to restrict expansion in market supply through the growth of the industry, limiting increases to those resulting from greater intensity of use of the existing (pre-zoning) stock.

The consequences of status quo zoning, therefore, may be determined by comparison of Figures III and V. The market price of vegetables will be higher, and the supply smaller, than in the absence of controls (Figures Va and IIIa). Zoned vegetable farms will be used more intensely and will command higher rents and capital values (Figures Vb and IIIb). There will be a number of wheat farms which, in the absence of the zoning restrictions, would have been converted to vegetable farming (Figure IIIc). Under status quo zoning, these farms cannot be used economically (Figure Vc). The rent, capital value, and intensity of utilization of all existing wheat farms are lower than they would have been (Figures Vb and IIIb). Further, the market supply of wheat is greater and its price lower (Figures Va and IIIa). Finally, fringe land which would have been improved for wheat farming remains vacant and undeveloped, another inefficient divergence from the best use (Figures Vc and IIIc).

From this example, it is apparent that restrictive land use controls can, in the context of a change in market conditions, have widespread economic consequences. Seldom are these economic consequences given consideration in a decision to implement or retain a zoning plan.

---

† Editor's Note: The increase in demand for vegetables is assumed to be insufficient to induce development of vacant land (i.e., land lying more than dw miles from the region center) for vegetable farming, "leap-frogging" over the wheat sector.

The regulated response: overzoning zoning

Overzoning requires that any changes in land use be limited to "higher" ones than currently prevail. An example is the zoning of agricultural land for industrial purposes, a common practice in many municipalities wishing to "improve their tax base." The apparent intention of this type of zoning is to encourage redevelopment in order to produce a more desirable pattern of land uses than that which currently exists.

Unless combined with restrictive zoning (see the following section), overzoning has no effect on the operation of land markets. Again, using the case presented at the beginning of this section, assume that all improved land is zoned for vegetable farming: existing wheat farms are, consequently, non-conforming uses. All unimproved land is again assumed to be unzoned and, hence, can be developed for either use. Under these conditions, the land market response to a change in the final demand for vegetables can be evaluated.

As zoning in this case does not act as an impediment to land use conversion, market operation will be identical to what it would be in the absence of land use controls. The important conclusion to be drawn from this example is that zoning does not determine the economically most appropriate use of land - it merely determines whether or not such use will be permitted. Existing wheat farms where the highest and best use is wheat farming, given current and expected market conditions and costs of redevelopment, will remain as wheat farms even though they are zoned for vegetable farming.

An interesting parenthetic comment relates the legal requirements to retain non-conforming use status. If a wheat farm was to sit vacant and unused for the specified minimum period of time, or its improvements destroyed, it could not then be used for this purpose even though re-improved. In these circumstances, the land would have no value for wheat farming, and the landowner would either receive no revenue from the land or be forced to improve it for vegetable farming. The capital value of the site as a vegetable farm would depend upon the current market for vegetables and transportation costs - if the site is too far from the market, the land may well have no value to vegetable farmers, and would be left vacant even though it would be viable as a wheat farm. Only if the capital value of the land as a vegetable farm exceeded the capital costs of redevelopment would it be improved for the "planned" use. But the "approved" use is not necessarily the economic one. In all circumstances where non-conforming uses are the most productive and where sites lose their non-conforming status, overzoning will, thus, result in an economically inefficient use of the affected sites.

Now consider overzoning under conditions of falling rental (and, hence, capital) value of the "overzoned" use (vegetables). In this case, market conditions may indicate that some vegetable land be converted to wheat, but this is precluded by the zoning regulations. As a result, the land use pattern will be affected by the regulations and overzoning will be equivalent to status quo zoning. Comparing the final equilibrium conditions, one may conclude that the market price of vegetables will be lower and the market supply greater than in the absence of controls. On the other hand, wheat prices will be higher and market supply lower. More land will be used for vegetable farms than would otherwise be the case. Thus, whenever zoning constraints limit market adjustment, they will have economic consequences; when they do not, they are redundant.

The regulated response: directional zoning

Directional zoning refers to regulations which specify permitted uses (to the exclusion of everything except those non-conforming uses which pre-date the enactment) in order to impose an overall land use plan. We consider the case where the region is zoned exclusively for vegetable farms in the western half and exclusively for wheat farms in the eastern half: new development or redevelopment, except for the specified use, is not permitted.

Starting with the conditions of the preceding example (Figure II), the initial increase in the demand for vegetables will result in the same short-run market conditions as the unregulated response (Figure III), since this does not involve any change in land use. The intermediate- and long-run reactions, however, will be significantly different, as the process of market adjustment through land use conversion must now satisfy both economic factors and planning criteria. The gain in the capital value of vegetable farms will result in economic incentives to convert some wheat to vegetable farms: such conversion, however, is only permitted in the western half of the region. As this occurs, the supply of wheat will be reduced, causing a wheat price rise in the intermediate run.

The final equilibrium is shown on Figure VI. The land use plan (Figure VIc) clearly shows the spatial implications of directional zoning which are compatible with the plan. A greater (lesser) portion of the western half of the region is devoted to vegetable (wheat) farming than would occur in the absence of zoning.† Similarly, a greater (lesser) portion of the eastern half of the region is devoted to wheat (vegetable) farming.

Figures VIa and VIb depict the economic implications of directional zoning. As a result of the restrictions on land use conversion (together with rising transportation costs as distance from the regional center increases), the market supply of both commodities will be less and market prices higher than would have occurred in the absence of zoning. The capital values and rents for all sites will be higher at final equilibrium, and all sites will be used more intensely. The owners of a number of wheat farms in the western portion of the region receive an added bonus through the *zoning induced* increment in the value of their land. Conversely, the owners of a number of wheat farms in the eastern half of the region are adversely affected (relatively), as they cannot realize the increment in the value of their land the market would "pay" them in order to convert to a higher (economic) use. However, the capital value of both types of farms will be higher at final equilibrium.

The restriction on conversion will also create situations where increments in value can be realized by owners if zoning should be changed. For example, wheat land adjacent to the eastern periphery of the vegetable area might have a value in vegetables by an amount that exceeds the sum of the current value as wheat farms and the costs of conversion. In situations such as this, speculation on zoning changes may become an important factor in market transactions.

Incremental rezoning

Incremental rezoning refers to the situation which occurs when land is rezoned in accordance with changes indicated by market conditions. The market adjustment process is similar

† Editor's Note: If the increase in the demand for vegetables was great enough, capital values for vegetable farms may dictate their new development. Whether this occurs prior to the redevelopment of the western portion's wheat farms will depend upon the relative magnitudes of the capital values of vegetable and wheat farms, the capital costs of converting wheat farms to vegetable farms, and the capital costs of developing vacant land for vegetable farming.

Figure VI

DIRECTIONAL ZONING

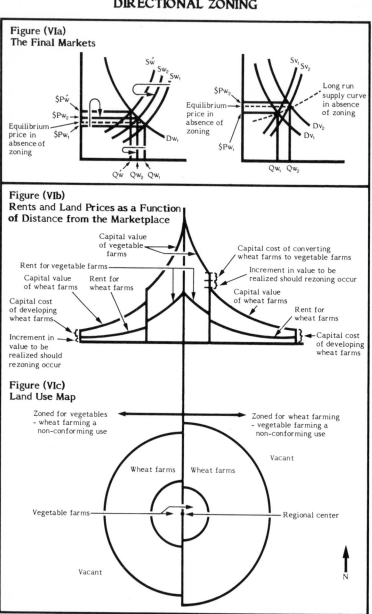

Figure (VIa)
The Final Markets

Figure (VIb)
Rents and Land Prices as a Function of Distance from the Marketplace

Figure (VIc)
Land Use Map

to that which occurs in the absence of land use regulation, but, unless rezoning occurs simultaneously with changes in market conditions, a longer period of time will be required for full adjustment to occur. This time lag will result in an intertemporal pattern of price adjustment for land with conversion potential.

Consider a parcel of land currently zoned, improved, and in use for wheat farming. As a result of a change in the demand for vegetables, the capital value of the site is assumed to increase in a manner which will justify immediate redevelopment. However, investors and landowners expect, on the basis of past trends, that it will be five years before rezoning will occur. These expectations will be reflected in the capital value of the wheat farm immediately, although it will be four years before the increment in value can be realized, as the following Figure indicates:

Figure VII
EXPECTED CAPITAL VALUE

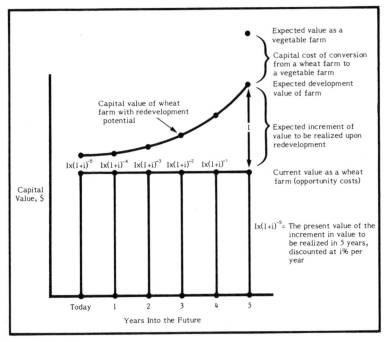

The lag in rezoning, therefore, will result in the land having a lower capital value than it would have if immediately rezoned and redeveloped, but a higher capital value than that justified by its existing use. This process of capitalizing expected future changes in value which will result from the removal of a zoning restriction is similar to the effects of expectations in the context of urban expansion as explained by Ricks and Weston[8] in their Life Cycle of Land Values hypothesis.

If landowners anticipate that the future removal of a zoning restriction will permit economically feasible redevelopment and land use changes, there is no incentive to undertake capital expenditures in maintenance of existing improvements that are unique to the current use unless they will result in a proportionate increase in expected revenue during the period before redevelopment. Consequently, many transition zones are characterized by disinvestment in current improvements prior to redevelopment. This is often characterized by a physical deterioration of existing improvements.

V. CONCLUSIONS

The preceding discussion outlined the characteristics of the operation of land markets in both the presence and absence of land use controls. It is apparent that land use controls have both direct and indirect effects on land uses, rents and prices, the extent of development and redevelopment, and on the prices and supplies of commodities to consumers.

The examples used in the evaluation were extremely simple, relative to the complexity of contemporary zoning and land use regulation that prevails in most urban regions. These models are valuable, nevertheless, for they isolate the consequences of land use regulation from the multiplicity of other factors which influence market operation. Although not exhaustive, economic analysis does provide one method of evaluating the market consequences of zoning in terms of the allocation of land uses, the supply and price of consumer goods, and the distribution of incomes or wealth, of such interventions.

This appendix has presented a conceptual framework for the evaluation of the economic effects of land use zoning. Many further aspects may be analysed using such a framework. For example, the concept of transfer of development rights (TDR) may be characterized as increasing the permitted density on a site previously zoned for a density below † that which was economically viable in exchange for a reduction of the permitted density of redevelopment on another site. By incorporating these characterstics into this framework, market and land use implications of TDRs may be evaluated.

---

† Editor's note: If the benefitting site is not underzoned, there is no incentive for the transfer of development rights.

Notes

1   Richard Muth, *Cities and Housing*, pp. 2-3.

2   Bernard H. Siegan, *Land Use Without Zoning.*

3   D. Ricardo and J.H. von Thunen, "On the Principles of Political Economy and Taxation."

4   W. Alonso, *Location and Land Use: Toward a General Theory of Land Rent.*

5   Recent criticism of Alonso's model may be found in M.R. Straszheim, *An Econometric Analysis of the Urban Housing Market*, and J.F. Kain and J.M. Quigley, *Housing Markets and Racial Discrimination.*

6   In the absence of non-market policies which accord differential treatment to owner-occupiers, such an assumption is realistic, since owner-occupiers will pay an imputed rent, equal to the actual amount of rent they forego by using their own land rather than renting it to a tenant (e.g., if you use your own property, you lose the rent).

7   The transport costs for non-land inputs can easily be incorporated. However, in order to preserve the simplicity of presentation, this added degree of realism is omitted.

8   R.B. Ricks and J.F. Weston, "Land as a Growth Investment," pp. 69-78.

ZONING
ITS COSTS AND RELEVANCE
FOR THE 1980s

Bibliography

Alonso, William. *Location and Land Use: Toward a General Theory of Land Rent.* Cambridge: Harvard University Press, 1964.

Baker, Jonathan. "Runaway Zoning." *The Vancouver Sun*, March 9, 1978.

Brigham, Eugene F. "The Determinants of Residential Land Values." *Land Economics*, Vol. XLI, No. 4, 1965, pp. 325-334.

Cheney, C. "Removing Social Barriers by Zoning." *Survey*, XLIV, May 22, 1920, p. 276.

Courant, Paul N. "On the Effect of Fiscal Zoning on Land and Housing Values." *Journal of Urban Economics*, 1976, pp. 88-94.

Crecine, John P.; Otto A. Davis, and John E. Jackson. "Urban Property Markets: Some Empirical Results and their Implications for Municipal Zoning." *The Journal of Law and Economics*, Vol. X, October 1967, pp. 79-99.

Davis, Otto A. "Economic Elements in Municipal Zoning Decisions." *Land Economics*, Vol. XXXIX, November 1963, pp. 375-386.

Davis, Otto A. and Andrew B. Whinston. "The Economics of Complex Systems: The Case of Municipal Zoning." *Kyklos*, No. 17, 1964, pp. 419-445.

Delafons, J. *Land Use Controls in the United States.* Cambridge: Joint Center for Urban Studies of the Massachusetts Institute of Technology and Harvard University, 1962.

Egger, Gerald. "Business and Zoning." *Houston Post*, September 6, 1970.

Ellickson, Robert C. "Alternatives to Zoning: Covenants, Nuisance Rules, and Fines as Land Use Controls." *The University of Chicago Law Review*, Vol. 40, No. 4, Summer 1973, pp. 681-781.

Ervin, David E., et al. *Land Use Control: Evaluating Economic and Political Effects.* Cambridge: Ballinger Publishing Company, 1977.

Fischel, William A. "A Property Rights Approach to Municipal Zoning." *Land Economics*, Vol. 54, No. 1, February 1978, pp. 64-81.

Gaines, John. "Deed Restrictions Termed Successful." *Houston Post*, July 12, 1970.

Goldberg, Michael A. "Land Use Controls: A Brief History and a Look Ahead." Mimeograph. Vancouver, B.C.: Faculty of Commerce and Business Administration, University of British Columbia, 1973.

Goodall, B. "Some Effects of Legislation on Land Values." *Regional Studies*, Vol. 4. Pergamon Press, Great Britain, 1970, pp. 11-23.

Goodman, William I., ed., and Eric C. Freund, assistant ed. *Principles and Practices of Urban Planning.* Washington, D.C.: International City Managers Association, 1968.

Heiser, Ronald A. "Houston: Giant of the Gulf Coast." *ASPO Newsletter*, February/March 1967, pp. 29-36.

Hurley, Marvin. "The Volunteer Sector in Houston." *Planning, 1967*, pp. 259-265.

Jacobs, Jane. *The Death and Life of Great American Cities.* New York: Random House, 1961.

James, Franklin J., Jr., and O.D. Windsor. "Fiscal Zoning, Fiscal Reform and Exclusionary Land Use Controls." *Journal of American Institute of Planners*, Vol. 45, No. 2, April 1976, pp. 130-141.

Jones, Roscoe H. "City Planning in Houston Without Zoning." Unpublished paper, 11 pages, Houston, 1977.

Kain, John F., and J.M. Quigley. *Housing Markets and Racial Discrimination: A Microeconomic Analysis.* New York: National Bureau of Economic Research, 1975.

Krasnowiecki, Jan I. "The Basic System of Land Use Control: Legislative Preregulation v. Administrative Discretion," *The New Zoning: Legal, Administrative and Economic Concepts and Techniques*, ed. by N. Marcus and M. Groves, pp. 3-13. New York: Praeger Publishers, 1970.

Lewis, Harold M. *Planning the Modern City.* Vol.1. New York: J. Wiley, 1949.

Madden, Daniel M. "Houston Holds Fast to No-Zoning Policy; Planners Content." *New York Times*, May 14, 1972.

Mandel, David J. "Zoning Laws - The Case for Repeal." *The Freeman*, July 1972, pp. 437-443.

Mandelker, Daniel R. "The Basic Philosophy of Zoning: Incentive or Restraint?" *The New Zoning: Legal, Administrative and Economic Concepts and Techniques*, ed. by N. Marcus and M. Groves, pp. 14-22. New York: Praeger Publishers, 1970.

Marcus, Norman, ed., and M. Groves. *The New Zoning: Legal, Administrative and Economic Concepts and Techniques.* New York: Praeger Publishers, 1970.

Maser, Steven M.; William H. Riker, and Richard N. Rosett. "The Effects of Zoning and Externalities on the Price of Land: An Empirical Analysis of Monroe County, New York." *The Journal of Law and Economics*, Vol. XX (1), April 1977, pp. 111-132.

Miller, Tommy. "Deed Restrictions: The Key Issue in Court Fights by Subdivision." *Houston Chronicle*, December 22, 1975.

Mills, Edwin S., and Wallace E. Oates. *Fiscal Zoning and Land Use Controls: The Economic Issues.* Lexington, Mass.: D.C. Heath and Company, 1975.

Moore, Peter. "Zoning and Neighbourhood Change in the Annex in Toronto, 1900-1970." Unpublished Ph.D. thesis, Department of Geography, University of Toronto, 1978.

Muth, Richard. *Cities and Housing: The Spatial Pattern of Urban Residential Land Use.* Chicago: University of Chicago Press, 1969.

Natoli, Salvatore J. "Zoning and the Development of Urban Land Use Patterns." *Economic Geography*, No. 47, 1971, pp. 171-184.

O'Harrow, Dennis. "Zoning: What's the Good of it?" *ASPO Newsletter*, Vol. 30, No. 7, July/August, 1964.

Ohis, James C., et al. "The Effect of Zoning on Land Value." *Journal of Urban Economics*, Vol. 1, 1974, pp. 428-444.

Olson, William A. "Alternatives to Zoning - The Houston Story." ASPO National Planning Conference, Shamrock Hilton Hotel, Houston, Texas, April 3, 1967.

_____. "City Participation in the Enforcement of Private Deed Restrictions." ASPO National Planning Conference, *Planning, 1967*, pp. 266-270.

Pierce, Neal R. "Will Zoning be the Dinosaur of the '70's?" *The Atlanta Constitution*, May 31, 1977.

Porter, Brian. "The Land Use Contract." Unpublished M.A. thesis, School of Community and Regional Planning, University of British Columbia, 1973.

Ragsdale, John W., Jr., "Constitutional Approaches to Metropolitan Planning." *The Urban Lawyer*, Vol. 5, No. 4, Fall 1973, pp. 447-471.

Reps, John W. "Requiem for Zoning." ASPO National Planning Conference, *Planning, 1964*, pp. 56-67.

Ricardo, D., and J.H. von Thunen. "On the Principles of Political Economy and Taxation." *Works and Correspondence of David Ricardo*, ed. by Piero Sraffa. Cambridge: Cambridge University Press, 1951.

Ricks, R.B., and J.F. Weston. "Land as a Growth Investment." *Financial Analysts Journal*, July/August 1966, pp. 69-78.

Roberts, John J. "Zoning - A Case Study." *The Freeman*, December 1968, pp. 721-728.

Rueter, Frederick H. "Externalities in Urban Property Markets: An Empirical Test of the Zoning Ordinance of Pittsburgh." *The Journal of Law and Economics*, Vol. XVI (2), October 1973, pp. 313-350.

Sagalyn, Lynne B., and George Sternlieb. *Zoning and Housing Costs: The Impact of Land-Use Controls on Housing Price.* New Brunswick, N.J.: Center for Urban Policy Research, Rutgers University, State University of New Jersey, 1972.

Scott, Randall W., ed. *Management and Control of Growth: Issues, Techniques, Problems, Trends.* Washington, D.C.: The Urban Land Institute, 1975.

_____. "Traditional Systems: Issues and Dilemmas," in *Management and Control of Growth.* Vol. 1, pp. 179-186. Washington, D.C.: The Urban Land Institute, 1975.

Sennholz, Hans F. "Radical Economics - Old and New." *The Freeman,* March 1971, pp. 147-153.

Seymour, David Ray. "Analysis of the Effects of Zoning Changes on Property Values in Two Pittsburgh Suburbs." *Dissertation Abstracts B,* Vol. 27 (1967), University of Pittsburgh, p. 4442.

Siegan, Bernard H. "Non-Zoning in Houston." *The Journal of Law and Economics,* Vol.XIII (1), April 1970, pp. 71-147.

_____. "The Houston Solution: The Case for Removing Public Land-Use Controls." *Land Use Controls Quarterly,* Vol. 4, No. 3, Summer 1970, pp. 1-19.

_____. "Zoning and Non-Zoning: Trends and Problems." A talk delivered at the Madison Hotel, Washington, D.C., May 12, 1971, under the sponsorship of the University of Chicago Law School and the *Journal of Law and Economics.*

_____. *Land Use Without Zoning.* Lexington, Mass.: D.C. Heath and Company, 1972.

_____. "The Continuing Efforts to Destroy Property Rights." *The Freeman,* 1975, pp. 46-47.

_____. "Zoning Misuses Land and Other Resources." *The Freeman,* 1975, pp. 461-462.

Sparks, Bertel M. "Changing Concepts of Private Property." *The Freeman,* October 1971, pp. 583-598.

Sparks, John C. *Urban Renewal - Opportunity for Land Piracy.* 1963 Essays on Liberty. Irvington-on-Hudson, N.Y.: The Foundation for Economic Education, 1963, pp. 51-68.

_____. *Zoned or Owned?* Essays on Liberty. Irvington-on-Hudson, N.Y.: The Foundation for Economic Education, 1965, pp. 101-119.

Straszheim, Mahlon R. *An Econometric Analysis of the Urban Housing Market.* New York: National Bureau of Economic Research, 1975.

Stull, William J. "Community Environment, Zoning, and the Market Value of Single Family Homes." *The Journal of Law and Economics,* Vol. XVIII (2), October 1975, pp. 535-557.

Toll, Seymour I. *Zoned American.* New York: Grossman, 1969.

Tunnicliffe, Kenneth W. "The Effect of Rezonings on Property Values: A Theoretical and Empirical Examination of the Taxation of Land Value Increments Attributable to Rezonings in the City of Vancouver." M.Sc. thesis, Faculty of Commerce and Business Administration, University of British Columbia, 1975.

Welch, Louie. "The Strength of Planning in Houston." *Planning, 1967*, pp. 253-259.

Wood, Rob. "Houston Apparently Can Survive Without Zoning." *Houston Chronicle*, November 30, 1977.

Woolfe, Donald A. "Zoning is Doing Planning In." *Practicing Planner*, June 1976, pp. 10-13.

the fraser institute

Member of the Association of Canadian Publishers and the Canadian Booksellers Association

Housing & Land Economics Series

PUBLIC PROPERTY?
The Habitat Debate Continued

Essays on the price, ownership and government of land. Edited by **Lawrence B. Smith,** Associate Chairman, Department of Political Economy University of Toronto and **Michael Walker,** Director of the Fraser Institute.

Twelve Canadian economists examine the operation and importance of land markets and the impact of government regulation, control and ownership on the supply and price of land. Essential reading for all those concerned with the future of landownership in Canada.

Contributors include: **David Nowlan** of the University of Toronto (on the land market and how it works); **Larry R. G. Martin** of the University of Waterloo (on the impact of government policies on the supply and price of land for urban development); **Stanley W. Hamilton** and **David E. Baxter,** both of the University of British Columbia (on government ownership and the price of land); **Jack Carr** and **Lawrence Smith,** both of the University of Toronto (on public land banking and the price of land); **James R. Markusen** and **David T. Scheffman,** both of the University of Western Ontario (on ownership concentration in the urban land market); **Stuart McFadyen** of the University of Alberta and **Robert Hobart** of the Ministry of State for Urban Affairs (on the foreign ownership of Canadian land) and **Michael A. Goldberg** of the University of British Columbia (on housing and land prices in Canada and the U.S.).

278 pages   7 charts   20 tables
$5.95 paperback ISBN 0-88975-014-9 $12.95 hardcover ISBN 0-88975-017-3

PROFITS IN THE REAL ESTATE INDUSTRY

A controversial question never far from the headlines is the subject of profits in the real estate industry. In this book, **Basil Kalymon** of the University of Toronto's Faculty of Management Studies concludes that profits in real estate do not significantly deviate from those earned in investments in other industries. Kalymon examines the question in a scholarly and highly readable manner and vigorously enters the debate on equity compensation and the comparative performance of publicly-owned real estate companies and developers vis-à-vis other sectors of Canadian industry.

59 pages   8 tables $2.95 paperback   ISBN 0-88975-016-5

RENT CONTROL—A POPULAR PARADOX
Evidence on the Economic Effects of Rent Control

Eleven essays on the economics of housing in Canada and on the effects of rent control in the United States, the United Kingdom, Austria, France and Sweden by Nobel Prize winners in economics, **F. A. Hayek,** and **Milton Friedman,** and **George Stigler, Bertrand de Jouvenel, F. W. Paish, F. G. Pennance, E. O. Olsen, Sven Rydenfelt** and **Michael Walker.**

230 pages   9 charts   28 tables $2.95 pocketbook   ISBN 0-88975-007-6

ANATOMY OF A CRISIS
Canadian Housing Policy in the Seventies

In this book **Lawrence B. Smith,** Associate Chairman of the Department of Political Economy at the University of Toronto, and one of Canada's leading urban economists, considers the content and objectives of Federal housing policies from 1935 to the present. His conclusions that 1) housing policy is more and more being used as a vehicle for redistributing income in Canada and 2) that this policy is at the same time destroying the private sector's incentive and ability to supply housing, make the book required reading for everybody concerned with housing in Canada today. The book contains a comprehensive bibliography.

55 pages   7 tables $3.95 paperback   ISBN 0-88975-009-2

THE DO'S AND DON'TS OF HOUSING POLICY
The Case of British Columbia

Economist **Raymond Heung's** book is a case study of housing in British Columbia. As well as taking vigorous issue with the methodology and conclusions of the Jaffary and Runge reports, (issued as a result of a B.C. government-funded Interdepartmental Study), Heung's book provides a useful and detailed framework for housing market analysis, together with an examination of the costs of adopting a housing allowance scheme for British Columbia. This scheme, guaranteeing access to basic accommodation for all residents in the province, would cost less than half as much as current government outlays on housing in the province. The book, written by a former staff member of the government study team, has a message applicable to every province. As such, it should be of interest to everyone concerned with Canadian housing economics.

145 pages   4 charts   28 tables $8.00 paperback   ISBN 0-88975-006-8

Books on Current Economic Issues

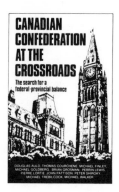

A timely
book on
Canada's
future...

CANADIAN CONFEDERATION AT THE CROSSROADS
The Search for a Federal-Provincial Balance

The eleven Fraser Institute authors examine carefully the extent to which the current allocation of powers and functions in the Canadian system of government serves the economic and cultural interests of all Canadians. Since the issues raised involve many aspects of our society, the book spans the broad mosaic of Canadian life from economic policy to legal uniformity; from broadcasting to urban development policy.

Canadian Confederation at the Crossroads: The Search for a Federal-Provincial Balance asks whether much of what is interpreted as **separatist** sentiment in Quebec in fact represents a deeply-rooted reaction to a rising feeling of alienation from government: a reaction as strongly rooted in the West and the Maritimes as in Quebec. As a solution, this book therefore looks at the ways personal and regional independence can be achieved within the framework of our existing constitutional structure. Can we produce a workable and acceptable federal-provincial balance that will reinvigorate our confederation?

Authors include: **Michael Walker,** Director, the Fraser Institute (Introduction); **Perrin Lewis,** Assistant Economic Adviser, Bank of Nova Scotia, Toronto (on the tangled tale of taxes and transfers); **John C. Pattison,** Assistant Professor, School of Business Administration, University of Western Ontario (on dividing the power to regulate); **Thomas J. Courchene,** Professor of Economics, University of Western Ontario (on the transfer system and regional disparities); **Peter Shiroky,** Fraser & Beatty, Toronto and **Michael Trebilcock,** Director, Law & Economics Programme, University of Toronto (on the uniformity of law); **Pierre Lortie,** Executive Vice-president SECOR, Inc., Montreal (on education, broadcasting, and language policy); **Douglas A. Auld,** Professor of Economics, University of Guelph (on fiscal policy); **Brian A. Grosman,** Professor of Law, University of Saskatchewan and **Michael J. Finley,** Legal Research Officer, Law Reform Commission of Saskatchewan (on law enforcement); and **Michael A. Goldberg,** Professor & Chairman, Urban Land Economics Division, Faculty of Commerce & Business Administration, University of British Columbia (on housing and urban development policy).

381 pages · 10 tables · 33 pages of extensive notes and bibliographical references · $9.95 paperback · ISBN 0-88975-025-4

TAX FACTS
The Canadian Consumer Tax Index and YOU

A major Fraser Institute book showing how the consumer tax burden in Canada has risen dramatically in recent years. Topics covered include *The Canadian Tax System; Personal Income Taxation in Canada; How Much Tax Do You Really Pay?; The Consumer Tax Index;* and *The Relative Burden of Taxation.*

By **Sally Pipes,** an Economist at the Fraser Institute, and **Michael Walker,** the Institute's Director, "Tax Facts" is a unique and highly readable analysis of the extent of direct and indirect taxation in Canada. In the case of some Canadians, hidden taxes make up more than 60 per cent of their tax bill. How much hidden tax do **you** pay? Do you want to know? Can you afford not to know!

The book contains a glossary of commonly-used terms, bibliographical notes and tables. It is an up-to-date sequel to the Institute's previous best-selling book "How Much Tax Do You Really Pay?"

140 pages	9 charts	29 tables	$3.95 paperback	ISBN 0-88975-027-0

THE HEALTH CARE BUSINESS
International Evidence on Private Versus Public Health Care Systems

Professor Åke Blomqvist, Associate Professor of Economics, University of Western Ontario, having studied the health care systems in Canada, the U.S., Britain and Sweden, recommends sweeping changes to Canada's system of medical insurance in *The Health Care Business.* In the process of ensuring equity in access to medical services, Blomqvist contends, the current Canadian system has become unacceptably inefficient and costly. The response of government to rising costs has been to increasingly intervene in the market for health services—gradually moving the Canadian system closer to the British system of "choice by bureaucrats". In the opinion of Professor Blomqvist, the result of this trend could well be a substantial reduction in the effectiveness of Canada's health services system—currently among the best in the world.

The Health Care Business sets out a series of changes to current medical and hospital insurance schemes in Canada which would have the effect, over time, of reducing the built-in cost escalation without materially affecting access to medical care. Blomqvist's recommendations are aimed at increasing competition amongst suppliers of medical services, breaking the conflict of interest that medical practitioners currently find themselves in and establishing an economically realistic basis for the delivery of hospital services.

208 pages	7 tables	$5.95 paperback	ISBN 0-88975-026-2

THE SCIENCE COUNCIL'S WEAKEST LINK
A Critique of the Science Council's Technocratic Industrial Strategy for Canada

The Science Council of Canada recently published a study by two of its researchers—"The Weakest Link"—which purports to prove that the root of the country's economic malaise can be found in the "technological underdevelopment of Canadian industry." One solution, the Council's book proposes, is the adoption of an "Industrial Strategy" based on "technological sovereignty" involving wide-ranging and potentially massive intervention by government in the country's industrial structure.

Because the Science Council's views on Industrial Strategy are acquiring increasing attention in government policy circles and what many believe to be a credibility that is undeserved, this Fraser Institute book, by **Kristian Palda,** a Queen's University Professor of Business Economics, represents a searching critique of what is becoming the "Science Council view"; as such, it is a particularly useful contribution to the on-going debate about one of the most fundamental issues of our time.

73 pages	6 charts	7 tables	$4.95 paperback	ISBN 0-88975-031-9

UNEMPLOYMENT INSURANCE
Global Evidence of its Effects on Unemployment

This book contains thirteen papers originally presented at an **International Conference** held in Vancouver. The proceedings begin with a broad, non-technical examination by the two editors, **Herbert G. Grubel,** Professor of Economics, Simon Fraser University and **Michael A. Walker,** Director of the Fraser Institute, of the relationship between "moral hazard", unemployment insurance and the rate of unemployment.

In Parts One and Two, the participating economists examine, empirically and theoretically, contemporary experience of national programs for dealing with unemployment in nine countries: in the **United States (Daniel S. Hamermesh); Canada (Ronald G. Bodkin** and **André Cournoyer); New Zealand (Geoff P. Braae); Sweden (Ingemar Stähl); Belgium (M. Gerard, Herbert Glejser** and **J. Vuchelen); Ireland (Brendan M. Walsh); France (Emil-Maria Claassen** and **Georges Lane); Federal Republic of Germany (H. König** and **Wolfgang Franz);** and **Italy, (Paolo Onofri** and **Anna Stagni).**

In Part Three, to add an historical perspective, two papers examine British social insurance systems—the 19th century Poor Laws **(Stephen T. Easton)** and the unemployment relief of the 1918-1939 inter-war period **(Daniel K. Benjamin** and **Levis A. Kochin).** This Part also contains an econometric study of unemployment insurance programs across a number of countries **(Dennis Maki** and **Zane Spindler).**

In addition to the delivered papers, the book contains provocative discussions by an international roster of economists who commented on the formal proceedings: **Melvin Reder; Erwin Diewert; John Helliwell; Stephen M. Hills; Michel Bergeron; Joseph E. Hight; Angus Maddison; Ernst Berndt; Louis Jacobson; Martin Feldstein; Samuel Brittan** and **John Cragg.** The informal discussions are summarized by **Sandra S. Christensen.**

400 pages	21 charts	18 pages of extensive bibliographical references and notes
82 tables		$14.95 paperback

ISBN 0-88975-008-4

PROVINCIAL GOVERNMENT BANKS
A Case Study of Regional Response to National Institutions

Can national financial institutions, such as banks, function in a country as regionally diverse as Canada without seeming to discriminate between the regions? Were the complaints of the four Western Premiers at the Western Economic Opportunities Conference in Calgary justified? If there is discrimination, would the proposed provincial government "B.C. Savings and Trust" super bank provide relief from it? What would be the cost of such relief? This book, by **John Benson** of the Economics Department at the University of Guelph, considers a very real and specific aspect of the sharing of regulatory power within Confederation. Professor Benson was invited by the Fraser Institute to examine the B.C. super bank to see to what extent it is justified. His case study provides a useful contribution to the current debate about the regional impact of national institutions and should commend itself to all Canadians concerned with the economics of Confederation.

136 pages   12 tables $3.95 paperback   ISBN 0-88975-020-3

THE REAL COST OF THE BC MILK BOARD
A Case Study in Canadian Agricultural Policy

Two Simon Fraser University professors of economics, **Herbert Grubel** and **Richard Schwindt,** analyze the social cost of the B.C. milk marketing board, the impact of the milk quota system and the extent to which the Board transfers income from consumers to producers. Grubel and Schwindt develop an analytical framework that can be applied to marketing boards in general. Their study documents the consequences of marketing boards and has been published to stimulate public discussion of the important economic issues at stake.

78 pages   6 charts   6 appendices $3.95 paperback   ISBN 0-88975-013-0

HOW MUCH TAX DO YOU REALLY PAY?
Introducing the Canadian Consumer Tax Index

Have you ever stopped to think what you pay your federal, provincial, and municipal governments in taxes? Have you ever wondered how much hidden tax you pay on all of the things you buy? This Fraser Institute Guide asks and answers two basic questions: Q: Who pays for government? (A: You do!) and Q: How much do you pay? By reading this book, you will see for the first time how astronomically the Canadian CONSUMER TAX INDEX has risen over the past fifteen years. And if you want to, you can actually calculate how much tax you really pay and your real tax rate.

120 pages   6 charts   22 tables $2.95 paperback   ISBN 0-88975-004-1

OIL IN THE SEVENTIES
Essays on Energy Policy

Edited by **G. Campbell Watkins,** President, DataMetrics Limited, Calgary and Visiting Professor of Economics, University of Calgary and **Michael Walker,** Director of the Fraser Institute.

In Part One, *Energy in the Marketplace,* contributors include **Russell S. Uhler** of the University of British Columbia (on economic concepts of petroleum energy supply); **Ernst R. Berndt** of the University of British Columbia (on Canadian energy demand and economic growth); and **G. Campbell Watkins** (on Canadian oil and gas pricing).

In Part Two, *Government in the Marketplace,* contributors include **Walter J. Mead** of the University of California, Santa Barbara (on private enterprise, regulation and government enterprise in the energy sector); and **Edward W. Erickson** of North Carolina State University and **Herbert S. Winokur, Jr.,** of Harvard University (on international oil and multi-national corporations).

In Part Three, *Oil in the Seventies: Policies and Prospects,* contributors include **G. David Quirin** and **Basil A. Kalymon,** both of the University of Toronto (on the financial position of the petroleum industry) and **James W. McKie** of the University of Texas at Austin (on United States and Canadian energy policy).

320 pages   17 charts   25 tables   index
$3.95 paperback ISBN 0-88975-011-4 $14.95 hardcover ISBN 0-88975-018-1

FRIEDMAN ON GALBRAITH
. . . and on curing the British Disease

Why is it that **John Kenneth Galbraith's** theories have become widely accepted by the general public when there is almost a total lack of support for them in the economics profession? Is Galbraith a *scientist or a missionary?* **Milton Friedman**, Nobel Laureate in Economics 1976, addresses these and other questions about Galbraith as economist and prophet in this Fraser Institute book. Whatever the reader's view of Galbraith, this book by Friedman is must reading. It is said that Canada and other countries are on the same path as Britain—to some, the *British Disease* is the logical ending of Galbraith's story. In the second essay in this book, Professor Friedman outlines a cure for the British Disease: the principles that Friedman develops in this essay are of immediate Canadian interest as they point out the necessity to adopt gradualist corrective policies *now* before the more jarring policies currently required in the U.K. are necessary here.

66 pages $3.95 paperback   ISBN 0-88975-015-7

THE ILLUSION OF WAGE AND PRICE CONTROL
Essays on Inflation, its Causes and its Cures

A look at the causes of inflation and an examination of responses to it in Canada, the United States and the United Kingdom. Contributors include **Jack Carr, Michael Darby, Jackson Grayson, David Laidler, Michael Parkin, Robert Schuettinger** and **Michael Walker.**

258 pages   16 charts   7 tables $2.95 pocketbook   ISBN 0-88975-005-X

WHICH WAY AHEAD?
Canada after Wage and Price Control

This book draws together the research and ideas of fifteen well-informed Canadian economists. It presents a remarkable concurrence of views on the controls program, its effectiveness and on the causes of inflation. The book suggests policies best suited to give Canada a healthy and internationally-competitive economy. It discusses the need for restraint in the public sector; it proposes policies to meet the critical double-headed challenge of low inflation and full employment. Contributors are: **Douglas Auld, Jack Carr, Louis Christofides, Thomas Courchene, James W. Dean, John Floyd, Herbert Grubel, John Helliwell, Stephan Kaliski, David Laidler, Richard Lipsey, Michael Parkin, Simon Reisman, Grant Reuber** and **Michael Walker.**

376 pages   5 charts   9 tables $4.95 paperback   ISBN 0-88975-010-6

TIMELY AND THOUGHT PROVOKING BOOKS PUBLISHED BY THE
FRASER INSTITUTE AVAILABLE AT YOUR LOCAL BOOKSTORE,
OR BY MAIL FROM THE INSTITUTE.

BOOK ORDER FORM

To: The Fraser Institute,
     626 Bute Street,
     Vancouver, British Columbia,
     Canada. V6E 3M1

Please send me:

_____ copies of _____

_____ copies of _____

_____ copies of _____

Please add $1.00 for postage and handling

Enclosed is my payment in full of $ _____ or charge to:

   Visa # _____

Mastercharge # _____

Expiry Date: _____

Signature: _____

Please send me information about membership in the
   Fraser Institute . . . . ☐

please print

Name: _____

Title: _____

Organization: _____

Address: _____

_____

_____

please include postal code